D[illegible] and Desires

Align Your Heart and Mind with God's Will:
A Daily Devotional

Decisions and Desires

Align Your Heart and Mind with God's Will:
A Daily Devotional

SARAH ADEJUBU

This is a non-fiction book. Any resemblance of the names and characters to actual persons, living or dead, is entirely coincidental.

ISBN: 978-1-0687803-2-5

Published in the United Kingdom in 2024 by
Framichi Publications.
www.framichipublications.com

Foreword

Written by Rev. Michael White

SENIOR PASTOR, THE TAB CHURCH
(London, United Kingdom)

It is with great joy and admiration that I introduce this heartfelt devotional by Sarah Adejubu. As a committed member of our church, Sarah has consistently demonstrated a deep faith and unwavering integrity. Her dedication to Christ and her church community has been a source of inspiration for us all. In this devotional, she shares her spiritual wisdom and insights, inviting readers into a space of reflection, growth, and deeper connection with God.

This devotional is designed to resonate with readers in a meaningful way, providing a guide for meditation, prayer, and purposeful reflection. Sarah has carefully crafted each entry to address topics that will easily connect with anyone genuinely seeking to strengthen their relationship with Christ. Through reflections on biblical principles such as reciprocity, fulfilling one's purpose, and cultivating courage, Sarah offers tools to help readers navigate their own spiritual journeys. One of the greatest strengths of this devotional is its accessibility. Sarah's words are not only meaningful but practical, allowing readers to take small steps toward integrating faith into every aspect of life. This devotional invites you to pause and consider what it means to walk with Christ, whether you are seeking renewed courage, clearer purpose, or simply a deeper understanding of biblical principles. Sarah's faithfulness and commitment shine through every page, and her ability to balance her professional career, and accolades, with a life devoted to Christ serves as a powerful example to us all. We are grateful for her loyalty to our church and for her willingness to share this gift with a broader audience. My prayer is that as you journey through these pages, you will be encouraged, uplifted, and drawn closer to the heart of God.

Preface

MAKING THE MOST OF THIS DEVOTIONAL: A GUIDE FOR YOU

Let's Explore the Word of God Together Through This Devotional! Feel free to engage with this book in any way that resonates with you. I recommend focusing on one chapter each day, giving yourself the chance to truly absorb and reflect on its message. Take time to observe your thoughts and behaviours with the guidance of the Holy Spirit. Each chapter is divided into sections, which are designed to enhance your journey:

1. Reading of the Day - this is the leading scripture for each day's message. I highly recommend you read this first before moving to the next section as it sets the focus for the message.
2. Devotional - this is the main reflection and study of the day. I encourage you to take your time to process the text. Give yourself the physical and mental space to read so that you can process how it may relate to you, and you can listen to

what the Holy Spirit is saying. Life can be busy sometimes but try not to rush through and take your time to truly process the message.

3. Meditation - After reading the devotional this is time for you to think and record your personal learning and reflections. Don't feel you are restricted to just writing, you can be as creative as you prefer such as drawing or mind mapping or using different colours.
4. Time to Pray - It is important for us to speak to God especially during our time of devotion. God is ready to hear our hearts and willing to change us. And so, you will find a list of prayer points centred around the devotional of the day. Feel free to add more or change the prayer points, the most important thing is that you are praying from your heart to God who hears, with the belief that He will answer you. I encourage you to continue to pray over whatever you feel or even have noted in your journal. Remember this devotional is your companion and I want you to use it in this way.
5. Scripture to Meditate on - You will find in some chapters I have included additional scriptures, the aim of this is to solidify your understanding in relation to the theme of the day.

As you embark on this devotional journey over the next couple of weeks, I want to encourage you to invite the Holy Spirit to search your heart and mind. This process can lead to profound self-discovery, helping you gain deeper insights into who you are and how you walk with Christ. The themes we'll explore together will prompt you to reflect on your spiritual journey and consider how you make decisions and where your desires originate.

Each day, as you engage with God's word—through its rich stories, inspiring characters, and transformative revelations—allow it to illuminate your path. My hope is that this devotional will not only deepen your relationship with God but also guide you to align your choices and desires with His will.

I urge you to fully immerse yourself in this experience. Take the time to be aware of your own thoughts, passions, habits, and behaviours as you move through each chapter. Consider how you would respond in the examples presented and reflect on your thought processes. This self-awareness can be a powerful tool for growth and transformation.

Also, remember that you're not alone on this journey. I encourage you to share your insights and reflections with others. Discussing your experiences can foster connection and understanding, and it might just inspire someone else on their own path with Jesus Christ. Let's embrace this journey with open hearts and minds, ready to grow and learn together.

My prayer is that as you go through each chapter, your desire for God strengthens every day and your decisions will align with God's word and will. May all the things that distract and lead you away from godly living be removed as you study and pray. And as the scripture promises, may God *"put His word into your minds and write them on your hearts; and He will be your God, and you will be His people" (Jeremiah 31:33)*. In Jesus' name, Amen.

May God Bless You.

CONTENTS

Introduction:

What Do Our Decisions and Desires Really Mean to Us?

Before you begin this devotional, I would like to explore what we define as our 'Decisions' and 'Desires' in the context of this devotional.

Decisions

Jesus instructs us to love the Lord with all our minds (Matthew 22:37). How we come to make decisions and the decisions itself, play a huge role in how we choose to love and live for God. A decision can be described as a '*a choice or judgement that you make after thinking and talking about what is the best thing to do* (Oxford Learners Dictionaries[1]). Our decisions can stem from our memories or how we process, imagine, think or reason, which are all so vital in our daily lives. For example, how we perceive ourselves and others, where we go, what we value. We have a mind and all that is in it is a gift from God. Through the Holy Spirit we can know what God wants for us and His mind for us (1 Corinthians 2:5-6). Having a renewed mind (Romans 12:2) as a Christian impacts our thought patterns of who God is, our perspectives on who God is, and how He both thinks and feels about us.

Our minds are powerful if it wants it could have the final say. After all, the Bible does say "*As a man thinks in his heart, so he is*" (Proverbs 23:7). If we love Jesus with our

1 https://www.oxfordlearnersdictionaries.com/definition/english/decision

mind, we end up giving Him control over our thoughts which allows us to surrender our will to His will and which then manifests in our decisions.

This devotional touches on the many ways we can worship God with our minds, through our decisions and obedience.

Scriptures to Meditate on: 1 Corinthians 2:5-6; Philippians 4:8; Isaiah 1:8; Hebrews 11:3; 2 Corinthians 10:5; Psalm 63:6; John 14 26; Philippians 3:12-15 *(Source: www.biblehub.com)*

Desires

Jesus instructs us to love Him with all our hearts and souls (Matthew 22:37). Our desires are deeply rooted as they affect and stem from our emotions, will, passions, affections, and what we are devoted to. It is the strong will to have something or have a longing for something. Our desires can be so strong that it can make us act in a particular way or feel certain emotions strongly. It drives our actions, choices, behaviours, and the level of intention on doing certain things because we believe it will create our desired outcome.

As Christians, our desires should ultimately be to be saved by God, to have a relationship with God and to please God through holy and righteous living. If this is our foundational desire, then the way we feel, think and act should all aim to coincide with this desire (hence the importance of exploring it in this devotional). The chapters in this devotional cover the diverse ways our desires can be aligned with God's desires for us yet also distracted and captured by the world. There are some desires that can show up to satisfy our physical appetites such as money, pleasure, or alcohol; but there are also desires related to power such as the desire to be in control, to dominate, to compare or to suppress. All of these have a way of secretly leading to sin, seeping into our Christian Walk and affecting our relationship with Christ.

Scriptures to Meditate on: Romans 7:22; Proverbs 3:5; Deuteronomy 30:6; Ephesians 6:6.

Relax! Don't You Know Who God Is?

Day 1

Reading of the Day: Psalm 104.

Psalm 104 is all about God's creation, sovereignty, and provision. We learn from this chapter that God's creation is perfect and purposeful in every way and provides everything we need at the right time. For example, we see in verse 14-15 that "He causes the grass to grow for the cattle and the vegetation for the service of man, that He may bring forth food for the earth, wine that makes glad the heart of man, oil to make His face shine." and the list goes on.

I want you to know that God has made provision(s) for everything in its perfect time and place, especially for you.

God the Provider

The animals listed in this scripture know their time, their place and that God is their provider:

- The birds know where to make their nests, they know where their home is. They won't go to the lion's den (verses 20-22) or into the sea (verse 25), but they know their God created the trees purposely for them to make their nests and homes.
- The lions and other beasts of the forest do not come out during the day when 'men go out to work' (verse 23 but at night. Meaning they know

their time and do not try to step out of it. When the sun comes up the lions go back to their dens, their domain.

- All of God's creation looks to Him for provision e.g. the lions "seek their food from God" (verse 21), 'He causes the grass to grow for cattle' (verse 14) and the springs in the valleys 'give drink to every beast of the field, the wild donkeys quench their thirst' (verse 11).

We can learn a couple of things here: There is an awesome power that comes with knowing God and who He is, that gives us confidence in our everyday life, it gives us a peace that surpasses all understanding because we KNOW God. And not just simply knowing Him but depending on Him and trusting Him fully. Psalm 104:27-30 reminds us of our reliance on God "They all depend on you to give them food as they need it. When you supply it, they gather it. You open your hand to feed them, and they are richly satisfied. But if you turn away from them, they panic. When you take away their breath, they die and turn again to dust. When you give them your breath, life is created, and you renew the face of the earth."

God's Timing

As God's creation, we must get to a place where we are content with God's timing because His timing is perfect for us. Imagine if the lions came out during the day because they felt like it or they reasoned that they could see their prey better when the sun is out. While that makes sense, it's not how God ordered it. He gave them what they needed to hunt in their own time. This is what we sometimes do - we make decisions because we think with our emotions or natural eye then conclude that our own decisions make sense but most times they don't and are also not aligned with God's timing (even when it looks like a great idea or opportunity). Imagine if lions came out when we are on our journeys to work, not only would that be quite scary and pretty dangerous, but it would create a lot of disorder. But God's timing for our lives is perfect, intentional, ordered and should allow for things to run like clockwork. When we get in the way with our own ideas, impatience, self-reliance and/or relying on other people, this can mess His perfect will and timing for our lives up. We have to learn that there is a time and season for everything, and God makes all things beautiful as you can see in this chapter. So, I implore you to trust God's timing, seek Him and learn to be content in His plan. Don't move too fast or too slow to miss what He wants us to do or give to us. Remember God is good and sovereign.

God's Placement

In Psalm 104, we read that everything knows where its home and habitat is. God has created the earth and has intentionally made a home for everything. I encourage you to pray to be in the right place at the right time, no matter what 'that place' feels like. If God wants you to be in a certain place in life, then trust that's where you are to be, as that is where God's providence is. Let's not forget God is understanding, loving and patient, but He is still God, and we are to obey him.

So it could be that God is telling you to remain in that church, workplace, relationship, friendship, or school, and to make it your home. Stay there, for God has a plan and will provide you with all you need for that place for the amount of time He has (or wants) you there. He'll never leave you where you shouldn't be any longer than you need to be. Trust is so important to be able to follow God and the way to build trust is to be in step and constant communication with Him. God will give us the peace that surpasses understanding because sometimes we literally won't understand but know that

He does. In times like this I encourage you to draw on His peace and His Strength to be obedient and faithful.

As God's children, we are to trust God and rely on His sovereignty, provision, and wisdom. We don't know more than God, but we were created for His great pleasure (Revelation 4:11). Matthew 6:26-30 reminds us that as God provides for the birds (home & food) and beautifies the flowers, how much more will and does He do for us already.

Let's see God in our now, recognise His providence in ourselves and live with a great amount of gratitude and confidence. Remain content with what God has and where He wants you right now because trust me it is the best and only place to be.

Meditate

What comes to your mind when thinking about your Decisions and Desires after today's study. Meditate and add anything that comes to your mind to the prayer list below.

Time to Pray:

- Heavenly Father, I thank You for who You are, and I thank you for your provision, plan, and protection over my life. Looking at creation, I can see your perfect design and intentionally in your love for me.

- I ask for forgiveness for times I have been ungrateful or thought I knew better than You. Help me to trust Your plans and appreciate Your creation, remembering that I am made in Your image.
- Please lead me where You want me and fill me with Your peace and contentment. Help me trust Your timing and see the beauty in every season, as each moment is an opportunity to know You better.
- Your Word says, "You will seek Me and find Me when you seek Me with all your heart" (Jeremiah 29:13). If I'm not on the right path, guide me, as You promise in Psalm 32:8.
- I pray to rely on You, remaining sincere, honourable, and obedient, and to resist the temptation to control my own life. In Jesus' name, Amen.

Read and declare Psalm 100:31-35.

Scripture to Meditate on:

"Yours, LORD, is the greatness and the power and the glory and the majesty and the splendour, for everything in heaven and earth is Yours. Yours, LORD, is the kingdom; You are exalted as head overall." 1 Chronicles 29:11

"From one man He made all the nations, that they should inhabit the whole earth; and He marked out their appointed times in history and the boundaries of their lands." (Acts 17:26).

But who are you, a human being, to talk back to God? "Shall what be formed say to the one who formed it, 'Why did you make like this?'" (Romans 9:20). (Source: www.biblehub.com)

“Delight yourself in the
Lord, and he will give you
the desires of your heart.”
Psalm 37:4

(Source: www.biblehub.com)

It's All Going To Be Just Fine!

Day 2

Reading of the Day: 2 Samuel 2 & 3.

In Romans 8:28, Apostle Paul tells us "That all things work together for good to them that love God, to them who are called according to his purpose." This means that as you are saved as a child of God, not only do you have a purpose, but God will always make sure that with whatever you are going through, He will turn it around to work in our favour. There will always be a blessing, it will align with His purpose, and you will have reason to thank God for it. This also means that sometimes, God is working in the background, and it may not seem or feel like it, but we are to develop in how much we trust His promise to us in this scripture.

Today's reading of the day is a perfect illustration of things working together for the good of David and for God's purpose of him becoming King of Israel come to pass. In the story we pick where there is a continuing war between the House of Saul and the House of David. At the time David was only the King of Judah, but Isbosheth (Saul's son) was the King of all the other tribes of Israel. David knew He was destined to be the King of Israel (1 Samuel 16:1-13) but it took a long time for it to happen until this moment. During the time when David was fighting through a war with his opponent, God was working in the background through a disagreement between Isbosheth and his commander, Abner. Isbosheth accused Abner of sleeping with one of his father's concubines and Abner took great offence. To the extent that he said "May God strike me and even kill me if I don't do everything I can to help David get what the Lord has promised him! I'm going to take Saul's kingdom and give it to David. I will establish the throne of David over Israel as well as Judah, all the way from Dan in the north to Beersheba in the south" (2 Samuel 3:9-10). When you think about this, there were many different ways Abner could have responded to this accusation: he could have apologised and begged for forgiveness, resigned from his job in anger or reported Isbosheth to the elders. He could have even taken him to war himself but for some specific reason he decided to retaliate by making David King, which some people would think was an extreme response. This is what we mean when all things were together for our good, God in his creative power set things up so that David would become king through a method that only God can be praised for. It is not a situation that David had to get involved in himself, but God was working behind the scenes. Here are a couple more reflections we can take from this story:

- God is in every situation, fighting all our battles, even when we can't see Him or any results yet. I'd like to reiterate that trusting God is so important since He is Higher than us, so are His ways (Isaiah 55:8-9). He loves us and has planned a good life for us, so I encourage you to decide to believe in Him. Be careful what you say about a situation also, because if you believe God is involved, speak life into it, declare Romans 8:28 over yourself and watch God move.
- Abner was an unexpected helper for David because he was the chief commander in Isbosheth's army (David's opponent). This shows us that whilst God is working everything out for our good, He can use anyone and so I wouldn't want you to restrict your view of how God will help and lead you to fulfil His purpose and yours too in Him. For this reason, it is always important to pray for discernment, insight and understanding so that you can walk in step with God and not against or away from His plans.
- David said in Psalms 138:8 "The Lord will perfect that which concerns me," and this is what God did for David. Not only did David receive all of Israel under his authority as king but he also now had

the superiority to demand for his betrothed wife Michal (verses 12-16). God not only perfected his kingship but also his family. When all things work together for our good, we know and can experience God's perfection in every area of our lives if only we are patient and trusting.

Meditate

What comes to your mind when thinking about your Decisions and Desires after today's study? Meditate and add anything that comes to your mind to the prayer list below.

Time to Pray:

- Heavenly Father, thank You for Your love and that all things were together for me as I am called according to Your purpose, and I love You.
- Please open my eyes and heart, grant me discernment and wisdom in all situations. Help me to be in the right place at the right time. In Jesus' Name, Amen.

“Remember not the former things, nor consider the things of old.”
Isaiah 43:18

(Source:www.biblehub.com)

“Because He Is, I Can!”

Day 3

Reading of the Day: 1 John 3.

The Bible teaches us that God is love and so since we experience His love, we now have the ability to love others.

In verse 16 of today's scripture, we learn the importance of expressing 'brotherly' love. This is because we see that Jesus laid down His life for us and so we ought to 'lay down our lives' for others around us including our friends and even strangers. As we mature in our relationship with God, we begin to understand life is not all about what, how or when we want things, but, it is about giving and sacrificing our time, likes, plans and wants so that others can be considered, and be reminded of God's love through us. In the same way Jesus gave His life so that our need for salvation can be met, we should be looking out for others so that their needs are also met. Paul even covers this when speaking about our gifts and talents, "A spiritual gift is given to each of us so we can help each other" (1 Corinthians 12:7) and "Since you are eager for gifts of the Spirit, try to excel in those that build up the church" (1 Corinthians 14:12).

I once had a friend that invited me to an event that was quite important to her but honestly, I wasn't comfortable going to nor was it convenient for me to the extent I even got quite upset about it and I was about to cancel on her. But after some thought, I realised I was acting in a selfish way since I had the freedom to change my schedule for that day, but she couldn't at the time. I wanted to do what was convenient for me only, but love is about sacrifice and doing things for others that might not be comfortable but will help others (just like what Jesus showed us). This is a small example, but I hope it shows how the small decisions we make impact how we love others. I like how Proverbs 3:27-28 reminds us of this: "Do not withhold good from those to whom it is due, when it is in your power to act. Do not say to your neighbour, "Come back tomorrow and I'll give it to you" — when you already have it with you."

It is important to love in action, deeds and in truth, not just in words. I have learned that only then I can be assured my heart is in Christ and of Christ.

We grow to know God through love because He is love (1 John 4:16). He loves us by calling us his children (verse 1). We are born again through Christ Jesus and so "Whoever has been born of God does not sin, for His seed remains in him; and he cannot sin, because he has been born of God." (verse 9). Therefore, we have the power to do right, love others and overcome temptation. Do not allow the devil to confuse or weaken the knowledge of the power you have in Christ Jesus through negative emotions or traits such as pride, unforgiveness and selfishness.

So, because God loves us, we must love. Verse 20 states “If anyone says, “I love God,” but hates his brother, he is a liar; for whoever does not love a brother whom he has seen cannot love God whom he has not seen.” Aim to not close your heart to others that could be in need but instead practise uplifting others, forgiving others, and showing generosity and kindness, all with the help of the Holy Spirit. The only direction of consistent practice is towards us maturing in the act of love, one step at a time.

Meditate

What comes to your mind when thinking about your Decisions and Desires today's study? Meditate and add anything that comes to your mind to the prayer list below.

Time to Pray:

- I thank You God for Your everlasting and unconditional love, especially when I have chosen not to be kind, loving, or supportive to others. I'm encouraged that You remain consistent, loving, and forgiving, even when I haven't been.

- I'm grateful for Your Word, which teaches me what true love looks like. Jesus, You are the perfect example of love, and with the help of Your Spirit, I have a blueprint to become more like You.
- I ask for strength and an outpouring of Your love that is kind, sacrificial, unconditional, forgiving, and not self-seeking. I pray to be filled with the love of Christ so I can give and receive love freely.

"My soul clings to
you; your right hand
upholds me."
Psalm 63:8

(Source: www.biblehub.com)

Stay Focused!

Day 4

Reading of the Day: 1 Kings 5, 6 & 7.

Through the scripture we learn that God has a purpose for us all and He will be on the journey with us to make sure that purpose is complete. We see this in the lives of Gideon, Joseph, and Moses.

In 1 Kings 5:3, the Bible tells us that David could not build the house of the Lord because of all the wars and distractions that he experienced. He tried his best to resist all that came up against him but ultimately, he could not complete what he needed to do until "the Lord put his foes under the soles of his feet." You see, there's only so much we can do by ourselves, and it is God's strength we need to completely overcome every struggle, temptation and distraction we experience in order for us to keep moving forward and win in life. More than anything, this knowledge actually comes as a comfort to me. Knowing that I have someone in my corner helping me and guiding me through life. Knowing that when I'm feeling spiritually, physically or emotionally weak, God is there as my strength, coaching, guiding and fighting for me. I am also reminded that trials and difficulties are to be expected but the deeper I get in relationship with God day by day, I am able to keep pushing forward, increasing my hope and faith in who God says He is. Jesus said it Himself in John 16:33 "I have told you all this so that you may have peace in me. Here on earth you will have many trials and sorrows. But take heart because I have overcome the world." And so, I encourage you today, try not to give up whenever you feel that there are too many distractions or difficulties, God has already promised you victory. Seek out God, draw closer to Him so that He can guide you through and give you the strength and power of the Holy Spirit. Even further, the victory will not just be for ourselves but will impact the lives of people around us and even generations to come. We see an example of this in 1 Kings 5:2 where the completion of the tabernacle was passed down to David's son, Solomon.

Bonus Reflection on today's scripture: 1 Kings 6:38 tells us it took seven years to build the house of the Lord and thirteen years to finish it. This shows us that good things take time, so don't let impatience and frustration be a distraction. Whatever you are building in life, understand it takes time if it's going to be of excellent quality. Nowadays, we do not spend enough time building the foundations, scoping out what we are doing, digging down to our roots and clearing out what's not supposed to be there. This could be trauma, unforgiveness, pride, or addictions; all things that can delay or ruin what we are building now and for the future. It is important to allow

God to spend time working on us. Isaiah 64:8 says that God is our potter, and we are his clay; so allow God to mould and build you so that He can be your foundation and fill you with all that you need to fulfil your purpose. Everything needs a good and solid foundation including:

- Our Relationships (even our relationship with God)
- Our Career, businesses & finances
- Our Health

Meditate

What comes to your mind when thinking about your Decisions and Desires after today's study? Meditate and add anything that comes to your mind to the prayer list below.

Time to Pray:

- Father God, I pray for you to make my pace align with your pace, make me slow down or move faster to align with where you want me to be in life.
- Help me to build solid foundations in every area of my life in You, piece by piece and day by day.
- Help me to be patient as I serve and live for you.
- Thank You for your promise that if I seek You, I can find You and that you promise to show me the

best pathway for my life. When I'm stressed and emotional I find it harder to remain strong and to keep going. But thank you that in my weaknesses You are strong, and that's all I need, You, the strength of my life. May You forever be glorified in my life as God my Defender and Strength, God my everything. In Jesus' name, Amen.

Further Scriptures to Meditate on:

"But he said to me, "My grace is sufficient for you, for my power is made perfect in weakness." Therefore, I will boast all the more gladly about my weaknesses, so that Christ's power may rest on me" (2 Corinthians 12:9)

"I will instruct you and teach you in the way you should go; I will counsel you with my loving eye on you" (Psalm 32:8)

(Source: www.biblehub.com)

“But the fruit of the Spirit
is love, joy, peace, patience,
kindness, goodness,
faithfulness”
Galatians 5:22

(Source:www.biblehub.com)

Who's Got What I Need?"

Day 5

Reading of the Day: 1 Kings 5, 6 and 7.

Reciprocity can be defined as a 'behaviour in which two people or groups of people give each other help and advantages (Cambridge Dictionary[2]). As we remain on the daily scriptures from yesterday, we see reciprocity demonstrated with both David and Solomon because in order for them to get what they wanted, they had to give up something that belonged to them in return. Solomon had to pay for King Hiram's household's food and David had to make a covenant with Abner both signifying that there was some sort of exchange).

Throughout the Bible we see how God views reciprocity. Some examples can be found in the following scriptures:

- Luke 6:38: "Give, and you will receive, Your gift will return to you in full - pressed down, shaken together to make room for more, running over, and poured into your lap. The amount you give will determine the amount you get back."
- Proverbs 11:24: "Give freely and become more wealthy; be stingy and lose everything."
- Galatians 6:7-8: "God is not mocked, for whatever one sows, that will he also reap."

(Source: www.biblehub.com)

2 https://dictionary.cambridge.org/dictionary/english/reciprocity

Reciprocity can be seen through the act of giving and receiving, which both shows and signifies God's love, provision, and glory through His generosity. It can also help us on our own personal life journeys to fulfil our purpose. This is because we have all individually been given specific gifts, strengths, talents, finances, timeframes, and experiences that can help and bless others. Reciprocity opens the doors for us all to work and live in unity with each other and have all that we need because we are ONE body of Christ. So, whenever the opportunity presents itself, always be prepared to give freely because you'll always receive. It might not be at the exact time or in the exact same way you gave it, but God promises that we will always receive it if we have a sincere heart and good intentions by obeying Him (Luke 6:38). It's the right thing to do because our Father gives to us freely, without us giving to Him. He gives us love to the extent He sent His only Son Jesus to die on the cross, forgave us for our sins and purchased us with His blood thus giving us eternal life so we will not perish in death and sin. This is the ultimate love and gift God has given us, so we too must give in every way we can whether it is via money, love, kindness, patience, or mercy.

God uses people to fulfil His purpose and so we have to respond by cultivating a collaborative and reciprocal mindset daily. We are not created to live life isolated, thinking we have to do everything on our own. Honestly, we don't have all the ability to succeed solely on our own, we all have something to give, lead or support someone else with. Maybe it's today that you choose to go out thinking of who you help or give to today. The more you cultivate this, the more you'll see God's principle of reciprocity manifest in your life.

In today's scripture we can reason that Solomon could have decided not to continue the good relationship his father David had with King Hiram. He could have decided to do his own thing to gain respect from the people he was now leading and have his own agenda. But he decided to maintain peace. Not just because of what he could get out of but because it was the right thing to do. He saw how his father was not able to complete the temple because of the various challenges he faced and importantly understood "now the Lord my God has given me rest on every side, there is neither adversary nor evil occurrence" (1 Kings 5:4). Where God had given Solomon peace, he had every intention in maintaining and keeping the peace. Whatever God has given you, do all you can to maintain and sustain it rather than being distracted or following your own plans and desires. Maintaining peace opens opportunities for more provision and the ability to move forward in life. For example, you would have read in today's scripture how by Solomon maintaining peace this got him an abundant amount of resources to build the temple (including cedar wood and a significant amount of workers). Even his father David, kept peace with Abner, and this enabled him to take back his Kingdom Israel and his wife Michal.

Meditate

What comes to your mind when thinking about your Decisions and Desires from today's study? Meditate and add anything that comes to your mind to the prayer list below.

Time to Pray:

- Thank You Jesus for giving your life for me, You were the ultimate sacrifice and perfect example of what true giving and generosity looks like. Thank You for salvation.
- Lord, one of the fruits of Your Spirit is generosity so I ask that You teach me how to be generous and remain consistent. Bless me with a giving and sincere heart, without expecting anything

back, but because You have asked me to give, and You freely give to me.

- Lord, I pray for the power to overcome selfishness, greed, pride and unforgiveness. Your word says You have set me free from sin (Roman 6:18), therefore I pray for the strength to not fall back into it but to live righteously.
- I pray Father to be a good steward and to look after everything you have given me, whether it is my time, finances, people around me, my job, gifts, or talents.
- I pray that within the body of Christ, there is unity. So that we are all working together in Your name fulfilling our purposes, living in love which demonstrates love that gives and receives freely.

Further Scriptures to Meditate on:

"For you were called to freedom, brothers. Only do not use your freedom as an opportunity for the flesh, but through love serve one another" (Galatians 5:13).

"Now you should finish what you started. Let the eagerness you showed in the beginning be matched now by your giving. Give in proportion to what you have. Whatever you give is acceptable if you give it eagerly. And give according to what you have, not what you

don't have. Of course, I don't mean your giving should make life easy for others and hard for yourselves. I only mean that there should be some equality. Right now, you have plenty and can help those who are in need. Later, they will have plenty and can share with you when you need it. In this way, things will be equal. As the Scriptures say, "Those who gathered a lot had nothing left over, and those who gathered only a little had enough" (2 Corinthians 8:11-15).

"Owe nothing to anyone—except for your obligation to love one another. If you love your neighbour, you will fulfil the requirements of God's law" (Romans 13:8).

(Source: www.biblehub.com)

Remember this is about the principle of reciprocity, so giving can be anything you have. This includes your time, kind words, comfort, a skill, talent, gift, opportunities, money, prayer, or resources. Continue to pray asking God to guide and direct you on how you can help others.

“We can make our own plans,
but the Lord gives the right
answer.
People may be pure in their
own eyes, but the Lord
examines their motives.
Commit your actions to the
Lord, and your plans will
succeed.”
Proverbs 16:1-3

(Source: www.biblehub.com)

"Sometimes I Need to Get Out Of My Own Head!"

Day 6

Reading of the Day: Exodus 3 and Luke 1.

Jesus prayed that God would glorify Him, so that he will glorify God. Jesus came so that we may have eternal life. That we may know God and accept Jesus Christ. We bring glory to God by completing the work God gave us to do.

Every single one of us has a calling, with the Highest calling to be a witness and share the good news of Jesus Christ to everyone. But we also have specific individual callings that contribute to this high call. We see this in the lives of Moses and Mary (the mother of Jesus). Though their callings were different, we can observe some similarities in their calls and hopefully be encouraged to seek and fulfil our own callings.

In both Exodus 3 and Luke 1, we see that either God Himself or His sent Angel visits them both with an instruction of what they are to do, for Moses it was "So now, go. I am sending you to Pharaoh to bring my people the Israelites out of Egypt" (Exodus 3:10) and for Mary it was "You will conceive and give birth to a son, and you are to call him Jesus" (Luke 1:31). We see that when God tells us what to do, He is very clear and purposeful in His instructions. The issue we sometimes have is our inability to hear God. We can be so distracted by our fears, doubts, daily life activities or even our own desires, that we are unable to discern and attentively listen to God's voice. And so, it is important for us to strive to remain in the presence of God (through prayer, meditation, being aware of God's presence, reflecting on His Word consistently) so that distractions are limited. Now, I can't say we are all going to have an Angel appear to us (some of us may do), but the beauty of being saved is that we have God's wonderful Holy Spirit living inside of us. And so, we have direct access to Him every moment of our lives. Jesus said in John 10:27 "My sheep hear my voice, and I know them, and they follow me" so as we grow and get closer to God, endeavour to listen out for Him. Ask Him to help you to silence all the noise including any negative inner thoughts so you can discern and learn His voice. This includes our own plans and any external pressures and expectations; we want to get to a place where we hear and listen to God's voice first in all things.

Sometimes we can be so caught up in our own insecurities that we doubt and question what God has called us to do. If we are to be honest, we do this because sometimes it can be completely different to our life plans or may seem incredibly impossible. We see this with both Moses and Mary, Moses asked God "Who am I that I should go to Pharaoh and bring the Israelites out of

Egypt?" (Exodus 3:11). Furthermore, speaking from a place of insecurity he pleaded to God saying "O Lord, I'm not very good with words. I never have been, and I'm not now, even though you have spoken to me. I get tongue-tied, and my words get tangled (Exodus 4:10)". He also most likely had his own plan to continue to work with his father-in-law as we can assume he was more comfortable there since he had left Pharoah and felt that he was now with the right family. The scriptures tell us that Mary was already pledged to marry Joseph and so she too asked the angels "How will this be…since I am a virgin?" (Luke 1:34). We have to remember that God is our Creator, He knows exactly who we are before we even know ourselves (Psalm 139:13 & 16; Exodus 4:11). Before He formed us, He knew us (Jeremiah 1). Meaning He knows the gifts, the talents, the calling He has for us, and we must grow to the level of faith that we believe that whatever God asks us to do, that His plan is best for us. I encourage you today, don't think about the how, trust in God that He will lead you through as He did with Moses and Mary. He is the same God yesterday, today, and forevermore.

God is ever so patient in nature, especially as He knows that we can doubt and question how things are going to work out. We read that God gave instructions to

Moses, He told him, "Now go; I will help you speak and will teach you what to say" (Exodus 4:12). And the angel answered Mary's question saying that the Holy Spirit was going to come upon her. We learn here that God is always with us, no matter what. This should be the comfort we have to come out of our comfort zones and ultimately be obedient to God. Whatever He is asking us to do, He isn't asking us to do it by ourselves but by His strength and power, and also by the Helper, the Holy Spirit. So, hold on to God as you begin to walk in your calling.

God showed both Moses and Mary that He is the Almighty and all-powerful God in order to build and encourage their faith. For example, God had appeared to Moses in a burning bush, Moses himself said "I will go over and see this strange sight—why the bush does not burn up" (Exodus 3:3). This was a strange and unbelievable miracle that can only be from God. As a result of God demonstrating that He is all powerful and that His power has no limitations, this increases the faith of anyone who sees this. God tells Moses that He is the 'I Am that I Am' (Exodus 3:14), and that He is with him in whatever capacity he needs Him to be. Knowing Moses' nature, you'll read through the following chapters that God performed more miracles, I believe this would have increased Moses' knowledge of and faith in God, building his confidence and courage to do what was ahead of him "the people who know their God shall be strong, and carry out great exploits" (Daniel 11:32). In Mary's story, we read that the angel told Mary "Even Elizabeth your relative is going to have a child in her old age, and she who was said to be unable to conceive is in her sixth month. For no word from God will ever fail" (Luke 1:36-37) This is a miracle in itself that her cousin who was once barren becomes pregnant in her old age! If Mary had any doubts before, hearing this would have removed all of them.

Although Moses and Mary's callings are exemplified in different ways, we learn how God can speak to us. We can be certain to trust in Him because he both knows us and knows the plans He has for our lives. God is patient and faithful to strengthen us and guide us; and will always show Himself present in our lives through His word and miracles. We now have a choice on if we are to be obedient. We see Mary respond by saying "I am the Lord's servant… May your word to me be fulfilled" (Luke 1:38) then relocated in haste to live with Elizabeth. However, you'll see in Exodus 4 that Moses' journey to obedience was a little slower, most likely due to fear and doubt. This was not pleasing to God at all (Exodus 4:24) and it was going to lead to Moses' death. This shows us that unbelief can lead to separation from God. Here we see the importance of obedience and truly trusting that God will be with us. God showed Moses many miracles, reminded him that He is the creator of heaven and earth and that He will be with him to help him to speak. Yet despite all of this, Moses still asked God to send someone else.

This must have hurt God's heart as the Bible says God's anger burned against Moses. I interpreted Moses' feelings as him saying to God 'You've made a mistake, you've got the wrong person, I don't have the ability to help me to speak properly or deliver Israel." I know I personally have said and felt similar before and still battle these thoughts but really our doubts, insecurities and limiting thoughts are not pleasing for God to feel. So, I encourage us to endeavour to grow so strong in our trust in God that we do what He says and trust He's with us ultimately to allow our trust to worship Him.

Remember God is loving, and we are free to share our unbelief and fears with God and ask Him to help us overcome them saying "Lord I believe, help my unbelief" (Mark 9:24). And as He strengthens and equips you, it's your faith that helps you to rise and begin to do what He has asked you to do (no matter how small). Remember God makes no mistakes and is faithful to perfect and complete everything He has started in you. "Let us then approach God's throne of grace with confidence, so that we may receive mercy and find grace to help us in our time of need" (Hebrews 4:16).

So, for anyone who has not yet already been doing so: perhaps it is time to begin walking in your purpose, stop delaying things! It is the best thing you can do for yourself. I wonder if Mary had known God's entire plan for Jesus, would she possibly have tried to hide Him, or not want to have Him knowing she would lose Him? But God sometimes doesn't tell us the whole of our story for a reason and we have to believe that what God does show and tell us is for our own good (this is a deeper level of trust we should be aiming for, similar to the trust that Job, Joshua and Esther had). God's plan is too great to know at once and may include some parts that will be tough, but we will get through (Isaiah 55:8-9). For example, we know that Jesus' death was for our benefit, as through it He gave us eternal life. So even in our darkest times there can be purpose in our pain. Mary was obedient to God, every step of the way. She didn't know exactly why or what was to come but she moved when she was supposed to.

Meditate

What comes to your mind when thinking about your Decisions and Desires after today's study? Meditate and add anything that comes to your mind to the prayer list below.

Time to Pray:

- Lord, help me to overcome all the limiting thoughts I have of You. Thoughts that limit what you can and will do for me and thoughts that limit how I respond to You.
- Lord, help me to discern and become aware of all limiting thoughts that come to mind, and please give me the strength to take them captive and shut them down in Jesus' name.
- Confess your fears and worries to God, lay them at His Feet and let His truth take over. He will help you as He helped Moses.
- I ask You to show me Your calling and purpose for my life. Please quieten all the worries, fears, and outside voices so that I can hear You and You are only.
- I ask for forgiveness for the times I have lacked in faith and been slow to obedience. Increase my faith and trust.
- Believe that God's grace and mercy will overshadow you. In Jesus' name, Amen.

“How can a young man
keep his way pure?
By guarding it according
to your word.”
Psalm 119:9

(Source: www.biblehub.com)

“Who Do I Work For?”

Day 7

Reading of the Day: Ephesians 6:5-8.

We see in today's scripture that we as Christ followers are likened to being a bondservant. In this context, it can be interpreted that we are to be committed to God continually (as a bondservant is to their master), not for a salary or to earn something back. But simply because we serve God, our Lord and Saviour who is sovereign. As we serve God in our everyday lives whether it be at work, in a team at church, with neighbours or friends, it's important we do the will of God with the right intentions and with sincere hearts. Not through fear of others, eyeservice or being a people pleaser. Everything we do shouldn't be to please people because their reactions can determine our response. For example, if someone is disrespectful, you might not want to do any work for them, yet if they are nice, you might want to do more but it should not be like this.

The Bible instructs us in Colossians 3:23-24 "Whatever you do, work at it with all your heart, as working for the Lord, not for human masters, since you know that you will receive an inheritance from the Lord as a reward. It is the Lord Christ you are serving." If we change our mindset to think in this way, it will be much easier to be honest, consistent, and not easily moved, while learning resilience and how to endure. We need to get to a place in our spirit and mind where our work ethic and actions are not based on other people's opinions or treatment of us. We would feel free with less pressure when we are motivated by our love for God.

Our primary motivations for doing good should be less about us coming across a certain way, to win awards or to receive praise from people but to reflect the love and work of God. Apostle Paul says in 1 Corinthians 9:25 "All athletes are disciplined in their training. They do it to win a prize that will fade away, but we do it for an eternal prize," he encourages us that eternity should be our key motivation.

Looking at the life of Joseph in Genesis (chapters 37-50), we learn he was a leader, an obedient son and good representative of his leaders wherever he found himself. He didn't change his belief, faith or his language depending on who he was with, he was consistent in serving God because He knew and trusted God. He knew God would always deliver him even though his location at times seemed to tell him otherwise. And so, wherever we are, it is important to serve God in truth and with consistency. God wants us to get to a place where He can trust us. He knows who we are and what we're capable of (1 Corinthians 10:13) and so we have the freedom to serve God faithfully. Sometimes life can feel mundane, or nothing seems exciting but even in those moments I encourage you to continue to be faithful, serving God with the right motivations and don't let your current circumstances determine how you serve God. Even if you're waiting on God for certain things in prayer, trust and serve God, remember everything God does is beautiful, purposeful, and not a mistake, Ecclesiastes 3:11 tells us "He has made everything beautiful in its time". This is truly serving God and living a life centred on God.

Meditate

What comes to your mind when thinking about your Decisions and Desires after today's study? Meditate and add anything that comes to your mind to the prayer list below.

Time to Pray:

- Thank you, Father, for your living Word.
- Forgive me Father for having the wrong motivations or intentions in things I do. Forgive me for any way I have served you half-heartedly as a way to simply please others.
- Father, help me to be humble and free from pride.
- Help me to be intentional with working to please You with a sincere heart.

- Help me not to lose sight that I am working to serve You on earth as You give me the strength to overcome all distractions and setbacks. Help me to always fix my eyes on You.
- Father, help me to aim to please You in all things and not man. To not only do things when people are watching or to receive praise for them. Or for them to control when or how I serve/work/help.
- Thank You, that You are the lifter of my head, and Your grace is sufficient for me.
- Father, I pray that I will remain faithful to you, no matter what I am going through. That I will always praise, worship, and serve you all the days of my life because I know that You are good, and Your ways are perfect. So, help me to always trust in you and hold onto You as my strength. In Jesus' name, Amen.

“You keep him in perfect peace whose mind is stayed on you, because he trusts in you.”
Isaiah 26:3

(Source: www.biblehub.com)

Faith and Pride: The Two Don't Mix

Day 8

Reading of the Day: Habakkuk 2:2-8.

The word 'Just' means to be approved. When the Bible tells us we are justified in Christ, it means we have been approved and accepted by God because our faith is in God (not in laws or through our works). True faith looks outside of ourselves and to the Lord, while pride always causes us to look within.

Our faith enables us to pray, praise, worship, and study the Bible, not through our own effort, but by the Holy Spirit working within us. We shouldn't be prideful about finding time to pray or study God's Word; it's God's will guiding our decisions (Galatians 6:14).

The best decision we can make is to give our lives to Jesus Christ. We can't boast about our jobs, accomplishments, or even our ability to be kind; it's all God's work and power at play in us. Let's thank God for His power and will in our lives.

Living by faith means trusting in God's timing, strength, and identity. In contrast, living with pride leads us to view ourselves as the source of our successes, leaving us perpetually dissatisfied and searching for more. We might ask ourselves what we can achieve next, how to please ourselves, or how to gain more money, accomplishments, or friends. When we follow our own agendas, our self-praise quickly fades and proves worthless.

God gives our lives true meaning and purpose. Hebrews 11:1 states: "Now faith is the confidence in what we hope for and assurance about what we do not see." The Message version highlights that "the fundamental fact of existence is that this trust in God, this faith, is the firm foundation under everything that makes life worth living. It's our handle on what we can't see."

The act of faith is what distinguished our ancestors (Hebrews 11), setting them above the crowd. Although we cannot see physically see God, we see everything He has and is doing, and so we are able to trust in Him. Without faith it is impossible to please God. Faith is just not about what we do, it is the foundation of our belief.

Therefore, when we believe our actions follow with humility! For example, Abel believed in God and so his sacrifice was accepted over his brother Cain's. Abel loved and believed in God. He reverenced God so highly that when it was time of harvest and offering, he was intentional and gave God his best. Which was the best portions of the firstborn lambs from his flock, whereas Cain just gave some of his crops as a gift to the Lord. He was not intentional as he failed to give God his best yet became jealous (pride) of Abel's sacrifice. Pride can lead to actions that are not pleasing to God, whereas living by faith allows you to honour God in the right way with your life because you see Him for who He is.

Meditate

What comes to your mind when thinking about your Decisions and Desires after today's study? Meditate and add anything that comes to your mind to the prayer list below.

Time to Pray:

- Father, I ask for Your forgiveness for not giving my all. Sometimes, I don't approach my giving with the respect and reverence You deserve. Instead, I treat it like a chore, and I do it mindlessly or out of pride.
- I also seek Your forgiveness for moments of unbelief and for not being content with what You provide. Please help me with my doubts and strengthen my faith. I want to serve You with the right intentions, in spirit and in truth. Guide me to give wholeheartedly and to trust in You fully.

"And I will give you a new
heart, and I will put a new
spirit in you. I will take
out your stony, stubborn
heart and give you a
tender, responsive heart."
Ezekiel 36:26

(Source: www.biblehub.com)

Looks God, But It's Just Not Worth It

Day 9

Reading of the Day: Matthew 4:1-11.

Jesus was led by the Holy Spirit to the wilderness and was tempted by the devil with opportunities that seemed attractive but were not from God. Some things may look like blessings, especially when they are things we think we need at that moment in time, but it is important to distinguish what is from God and what is not from God. For example, when Jesus was hungry, the devil tempted Him to turn stones into bread (which could represent lust of the eyes). When Jesus responded with "It is written: 'Man shall not live on bread alone, but on every word that comes from the mouth of God" (Matthew 4:4) we learn the importance of needing to know God's word and truth for ourselves. Thankfully, we have the Holy Spirit who is not only called the Spirit of Truth but the Helper (see John 14) who is able to guide us in all truth. The devil knows the word but doesn't have the Holy Spirit like we do and therefore we have the power to overcome all temptation.

With all the temptations Jesus encountered, He remembered His calling was to save us. Throughout His life on earth Jesus stayed on the course of His calling, He was not distracted by other things like His own wants, needs, or difficulties. Sometimes our own desires and wants can distract us from doing what God has asked us to do, such as loving others, sharing with others or putting other people's needs first. And we have to encourage ourselves to do the same, remembering that our purpose goes beyond being about just us.

Thankfully, Jesus has shown us how we can stay focused and overcome temptations; we see this in Matthew 4:8-11:

"Again, the devil took him to a very high mountain and showed him all the kingdoms of the world and their splendour. "All this I will give you," he said, "if you will bow down and worship me." Jesus said to him, "Away from me, Satan! For it is written: 'Worship the Lord your God and serve him only.'" Then the devil left him, and angels came and attended him" (Matthew 4:8-11). (Source: www.biblehub.com)

We can learn from this scripture that Jesus is the Word and whenever distractions and temptations arise from the enemy, it is important to speak the living Word of God (scriptures) to him. Just as Jesus did so to resist the devil, we can too. The Bible proves this by informing us that "the Spirit (of God) who lives in you is greater than the spirit (the devil) who lives in the world" (1 John 4:4).

Jesus who was fully God yet fully man had all the power to destroy the devil without delay. But God being so kind to us demonstrated that by using His word as our weapon we can overcome any temptations thrown at us by the devil. Jesus showed us in humanity once again how to live life in this world and that we do not have to fight in our own strength. Thank you, Jesus.

Meditate

What comes to your mind when thinking about your Decisions and Desires after today's study? Meditate and add anything that comes to your mind to the prayer list below.

Time to Pray:

- Heavenly Father, I ask You to renew Your power in me to overcome temptation no matter how often it comes.
- I pray for consistency in reading and understanding Your Word and for a strong memory to retain it. Please surround me with people who will guide me rightly and not lead me astray.
- I seek more of Your Holy Spirit in my life and just as Jesus showed me to pray always. I too pray to be more consistent in my prayer life.
- Thank You, God, for Your peace and for making me Yours. Help me to seek You and do what is right, knowing I can't do this life on my own.

It is important for our spirits, souls, bodies to be kept blameless, sanctified, and holy for God. It is not just about what we say, speak and do, but it's about our thoughts, emotions, motivations, will, decisions and desires. May all of us be kept blameless in Jesus' name, Amen.

Lastly, remember that we share the Spirit of God and despite our spirit often warring against our flesh, God has enabled His Spirit to always win.

Further Scriptures to Meditate on:

"For the world offers only a craving for physical pleasure, a craving for everything we see, and pride in our achievements and possessions. These are not from the father but are from this world" (1 John 2:16).

"I have told you all this so that you may have peace in me. Here on earth, you will have many trials and sorrows. But take heart, because I have overcome the world" (John 16:13).

(Source: www.biblehub.com)

“For God gave us a spirit
not of fear but of power
and love and self-control.”
2 Timothy 1:7

(Source: www.biblehub.com)

“I Still Matter”

Day 10

Reading of the Day: Luke 15:11-32.

Sometimes we can get upset or question why some non-believers have supernatural experiences or when some believers or even non-believers say things like 'Jesus revealed Himself to me in this way or that way.' You may have even questioned why you yourself have not experienced the supernatural or Jesus in a comparable way, thinking you are less special than those who have. If that has ever been you, my response to you today is 'You are already HIS! You're already part of His Kingdom saved by grace and you have full access to God, so never forget that'. This reminds me of the parable of The Prodigal Son. Let's go on a journey through the story (please read Luke 15:11-32 before continuing).

Firstly, in verse 12 we see that the prodigal son was the youngest son in this parable, and for the purpose of this devotional we can liken him to represent new Christians, unbelievers, or even immature Christians. Similarly, we can then liken his older brother to more mature Christians, or people who have been Christ followers a long time; with the father representing God our Father. When the younger brother says to his father (still in verse 12) "give me the portion of goods that falls to me", could this mean the immaturity in him wanted all the fleshly enjoyment and the benefits of God the Father without actually being with the Father? My opinion is that the prodigal son requested his portion of his inheritance too early, and his impatience caused him to make a rash decision without seeking any wisdom, counsel, or guidance. In doing so, he failed to see all the things his father already had in store for him for the future.

In verses 14 - 15, we see that with God, you can end up in an unknown and distant place far from Him, doing things you wouldn't dream of doing when you were with God. Verse 16 shows us that the prodigal son's appetite even changed, and began adapting to his new environment which was so far from where he came from (his father's house) and he didn't even know it, the scripture tells us " he would gladly have filled his stomach with the pods that the swine ate" (Luke 15:16). He was so deep into this life that he became hopeless and blind. People who aren't saved are also hopeless and blind, their appetite has changed so they don't even know that they should desire God and also "Taste and see that the Lord is good" (Psalm 34:8) – they are far from this. That's why they need to experience a life changing encounter with God (like Paul did in Acts 9:3-8) so their eyes can be opened.

We see in verse 17 that the prodigal son "came to himself" which opened his eyes up to his prodigal living/ lifestyle. God in His grace always provides an opportunity where He reveals Himself to us, especially when we have become distant and walked away from Him somehow. It is up to us to decide whether we draw back to Him or draw further away. But the prodigal son didn't ignore this moment, he got up and decided to go back to his father's house. God shows up for everyone but is even more found when we ourselves realise and admit how far we are from Him but desire to change. "When he was still a great way off, his father saw him and had compassion" (verse 20), the prodigal son's father ran and fell on his neck, kissing him. Likewise, God is always ready to welcome us back into His arms as the loving, merciful and compassionate Father He is. Just like a father kissing his son, God's love to us is immense and overpowering, feels extraordinary, and cannot be missed. Taking us back to the beginning of today's devotion, this is just one way people can experience a supernatural encounter with God; a moment where eyes are opened and minds are changed leading to repentance, coming back to God.

Next, we see how God shows people that their true identity is found in Him. I like how 1 Peter 2:9 reminds us that we 'are a chosen generation, a royal priesthood, a holy nation' and God's 'own special people'. The son went from being a citizen of a foreign country, wanting to eat the pigs food to wearing the best robe, clothed by his father, with a ring and sandals which represents belonging and citizenship. In a similar fashion, God does this with us when we repent. I like how Isaiah 61:10 puts it: "For he has clothed me with garments of salvation and arrayed me in a robe of righteousness." Wherever the son now goes, he is covered and has the identity of the kingdom he's from. The father now protects him, taking off the garment of shame and clothed him with the garment of praise (Isaiah 61:3).

The father in verse 31 (representing God in this parable) says to his older son "all I have is yours". It is important that we as Christians do not forget this now allow ourselves to fall into comparison. We should celebrate when someone becomes saved or has a supernatural experience with Jesus, as it doesn't mean you're forgotten or you're not special. God says to you today "you are always with Me and all that I have is yours." God says I'll never leave you nor forsake you" (Deuteronomy 31:8) and "my grace is sufficient for you" (2 Corinthians 12:9), knowing this and believing is all that matters. So, I encourage you (as I encourage myself) to stay close to God while maintaining and developing your relationship with Him and then you'll see and experience Him every day. Out of love and compassion celebrate when others are blessed and favoured whether they've been a Christian for less time than you or not yet part of the faith. We are all equal children of God and loved by Him. Every encounter from God is an opportunity for us and everyone around us to give Him the glory.

Meditate

What comes to your mind when thinking about your Decisions and Desires after today's study. Meditate and add anything that comes to your mind to the prayer list below.

Time to Pray:

- Lord, I thank God for Your everlasting, unconditional love (which saves and forgives), allowing me to be aware of Your nearness and presence.
- I pray to love people as Christ loves people.
- I pray to not be judgmental, self-righteous, ungrateful, nor forget my identity in Christ.
- I pray against comparison and unfruitfulness in the house of God.
- I pray for the salvation of the world, for unbelievers to experience You supernaturally so they come to themselves and see themselves as You see them. Name the people you know who need to give their lives to Jesus so they too can be saved.

“Set your minds on things that are above, not on things that are on earth.”
Colossians 3:2

(Source:www.biblehub.com)

It's More Than Money

Day 11

Reading of the Day: 3 John 1:2.

The word prosper means 'to thrive; to be a success; to flourish; have positive wellbeing, (Oxford English Dictionary[3]) so that 'all things go well' as today's scripture puts it.

Paul was praying for his friend Gaius, for everything in his life to prosper, just as his soul was prospering (you can see in later verses 5-8 how Gaius' actions showed he was growing and doing well spiritually through his level of faithfulness and love. Paul prays for Gaius' health and all areas of his life which could have perhaps included his finances, relationships, career, mental and emotional health, as well as his vision and purpose. In the times we are now living in, it is so easy for us to think prospering is only about having money and being comfortable financially. This is where I confess that this is what I used to think; that if I had money, most (if not all) of my worries would go away!). But throughout the Bible we see how vital it is for our soul and spirit to prosper in life primarily. If our spirit is healthy then everything else follows, meaning if we are following God and seeking Him first in all we do, God will direct us in all other things and provide for us in every way. As a reminder, Matthew 6:33 says, "But seek first the kingdom of God

3 https://www.oed.com/search/dictionary/?scope=Entries&q=flourish

and his righteousness, and all these things will be added to you". Seeking God first in our lives causes our spirit and soul to prosper and then everything else in life will follow, this is a promise from God. However, sometimes we only focus on what we want to do, following our own selfish desires or plans, instead of following God's design of living and commandments. Many Christians would be gravely ill if their physical health was instantly in the same state as their spiritual health. Romans 8:13 says "if you live according to the flesh you will die, but if by the Spirit you put to death the deeds of the body, you will live." The flesh is your sinful nature, it is what is apart from God and drives you to do things you know are not right and you know you do not want to do. The Spirit of God within us enables us to grow and pursue a holy and righteous life. Living in God's Spirit means living as a child of God.

Continuing in Romans 8, verse 16 says "The Spirit Himself bears witness with our Spirit that we are Children of God". And so, as God's children, our identity permits us to have certain rights and access to God so that we are led and provided for by Him. So, for anyone that is worried about succeeding or doing well in any part of their lives, be reminded of what Romans 8:15 says, "you have not received a spirit that makes you fearful slaves. Instead, you received God's Spirit when he adopted you as his own children." God's Spirit enables us to live a complete prosperous life, and it starts with our decision and desire to pursue Him today through prayer and trust.

Meditate

What comes to your mind when thinking about your Decisions and Desires after today's study? Meditate and add anything that comes to your mind to the prayer list below.

Time to Pray:

- Pray for forgiveness for living according to your flesh and not living in accordance with the Spirit of God.
- Pray to grow and be strengthened in your spiritual health - your habits, vision, purpose, level of understanding, wisdom, and for God to move over your life.
- Pray to prosper in your physical health, including for any healing and strength.
- Pray to prosper in your mental health, including for peace, wisdom, and discernment.

- Pray to prosper in your financial health, including for provision and increase and against the temptation of greed and selfishness. As well as for Godly financial wisdom to manage your finances well.
- Pray for God's grace and the power to be consistent, so that you can be consistent with all things and practices that help your soul to prosper and to have a good journey in life.

Further Scriptures to Meditate on:

"Now may the God of peace Himself sanctify you completely and may your whole spirit and soul and body be kept blameless at the coming of our Lord Jesus Christ" (1 Thessalonians 5:23).

(Source: www.biblehub.com)

"You will seek me and
find me, when you seek
me with all your heart."
Jeremiah 29:13

(Source: www.biblehub.com)

What Is Your Heart Showing Me?

Day 12

Reading of the Day: Matthew 19:26.

Today's scripture reads: "But Jesus looked at them and said to them, "With man all things are impossible, but with God all things are possible"'. This was Jesus' response to a question from a wealthy young man who felt he was living a life that followed God's commandments but wanted to know about how to have eternal life. Jesus responded to him by instructing him to sell all his things and give the money to the poor, only then will he have true treasures in heaven. When we think about 'treasures in heaven,' we think about Jesus, it is about increasing our storehouse to have more of Jesus in us. The more we do in life through faith, the more we build treasures in Heaven because it shows Jesus is our treasure. When we invest our time, money, talents to expand His Kingdom it shows that He is important to us. Notice that the wealthy man had followed the commandments, however because of his relationship with his material wealth, Jesus knew that his heart was not for God and therefore not his treasure. The more generous we are to people, it shows more of Jesus. It invites those who do not know Jesus to know more about His love and provision, which is a step towards their own salvation (in getting to know God). This is one example of how we can expand God's Kingdom and add to our

Heavenly treasures. 1 Timothy 6:18-19 encourages us to "do good, be rich in good works, generous & ready to share", and as a result, whoever does this "is storing up for themselves the treasure of a good foundation for the future that they may take hold of that which is truly life".

Doing good in the eyes of God really starts from our heart posture. If our hearts love God and want what God wants, it will desire to love others and change the way we see and treat other people (God's people). Our hearts can be easily offended; full of jealousy; have bad intentions; be plagued with disappointment and hurt or harbour unforgiveness, which then discourages us to seek and follow the way of [doing] life God wants for us - which is ultimately the plan of the enemy. For this very reason, Proverbs 4:23 encourages us to "Guard your heart above all else, for it determines the course of your life.".

Here are some examples of what guarding your heart may look like:

- Having daily prayer and Bible study. By feeding yourself with God's word you learn about His ways, and His expectations which can help to guard your heart from all unrighteousness. (Hebrews 4:12 & 2 Timothy 3:16-17).
- Ensuring that you are surrounded with the right types of people that can draw you closer to

God rather than further away, for example the conversations you have or how you choose to respond to things.

- being aware of your thoughts and taking captive the thoughts that are against God's Word (2 Corinthians 10:5)
- filtering what you say and do, our emotions, desires, and thoughts through God's Word.

The more we do this, the more we allow God to be Lord over our lives, enabling us to do good and be generous, despite what we may be going through or what we may be facing at the hand of others. This is what Jesus meant when He said, "With man this is impossible, but with God all things are possible" (Matthew 19:26). On our own we are too self-consumed, proud, and selfish to love people to the point we can forgive or put them before ourselves all the time, but as we are now saved and have accepted Jesus, it is His Spirit who lives in us. Let us be encouraged by Philippians 2:13 which says, "For God is working in you, giving you the desire and the power to do what pleases him." This is an encouragement to me as it teaches me that by guarding my heart, I can deepen and strengthen my relationship with God, enabling me to do good in His eyes and demonstrate His love. Remember Jesus said "Remain in me, as I also remain in you. No branch can bear fruit by itself; it must remain in the vine. Neither can you bear fruit unless you remain in me" (John 15:4).

Here are some examples of doing good:

- Serving, caring, and helping others
- Serving in your local church
- Sharing and giving to others
- Spending time with people
- Pursuing theirs & your own righteousness,

Meditate

What comes to your mind when thinking about your Decisions and Desires after today's study? Meditate and add anything that comes to your mind to the prayer list below.

Time to Pray:

- Thank You Heavenly Father for saving me. Lord You are my treasure, and I love You.
- I pray to not be conceited or proud, and to not to fix my hope on uncertain things like money, people, or status, but instead on You Father.
- Help me to be rich in good works, to be generous to others and ready to share always.

- Help me to store up treasures in Heaven so that I can take hold of that which is life, as found in Christ.
- Jesus, I ask you to search my heart, search the posture of my heart and forgive me for not seeking You, for being disobedient and for continuing in my sin. I repent of my ways and ask for You to cleanse my heart from all the things that are not of You with the Blood of Jesus.
- I pray Lord, that Your word will live and dwell within my heart, and may You strengthen me and teach me how to guard my heart with all diligence.
- Help me Jesus to be consistent with my prayer life and to continually study and follow Your word. So, I can filter what I say, manage my emotions, make the right decisions, and have the type of desires and relationships that please You.
- Thank You for Your patience, mercy, and grace Father. I need more of you Jesus! In Jesus' name, Amen.

Be reminded that God is our Provider, so this means we have all reason to be generous with all we have (including with our love, money & time) because God's well never runs dry.

Further Scriptures to Meditate on:

"For it was I, the Lord your God, who rescued you from the land of Egypt. Open your mouth wide, and I will it with good things" Psalm 81:10

"Command those who are rich in this present world not to be arrogant nor to put their hope in wealth, which is so uncertain, but to put their hope in God, who richly provides us with everything for enjoyment. Command them to do good, to be rich in good deeds, and to be generous and willing to share. In this way they will lay up treasure for themselves as a firm foundation for the coming age, so that they may take hold of the life that is truly life" (1 Timothy 6:17-19).

(Source: www.biblehub.com)

“Let the words of
my mouth and the
meditation of my heart be
acceptable in your sight,
O Lord, my rock and my
redeemer.”
Psalm 19:14

(Source: www.biblehub.com)

"I am Free!"

Day 13

Reading of the Day: 2 Peter 1.

As Christians, it's essential to remind ourselves of the foundation of our faith. Today's focus serves as both a personal reflection and an invitation to share our faith with others. From the very beginning, God's plan was for us to be holy and blameless as His children. Though the fall of Adam introduced sin and death into the world, God, in His great love and mercy, was not content to leave us in separation from Him. His plan of redemption was birthed out of love—not anger—and He made a way for us to return to Him, even though we didn't deserve it.

This restoration was made possible through Jesus. By His sacrifice on the cross—His death and resurrection—we are forgiven, freed from the power of sin and death, and redeemed. When we accept Jesus, we also share in His resurrection power, receiving eternal life and becoming heirs of God's promises. We were chosen before we were born, according to His divine purpose. Through Jesus, we are adopted as God's own, called to praise Him for His unmerited love.

When we accept Christ as our Lord and Savior, we are sealed by the Holy Spirit (Ephesians 1:13). This is God's guarantee of the eternal inheritance He has promised us, and the Spirit affirms that we are His, marked as His own people (Ephesians 1:14). The Holy Spirit empowers us to live in a way that glorifies God, fulfilling His will for us. As Romans 8:14 says, "For as many as are led by the Spirit, these are the sons of God." We are now part of the body of Christ, never alone, for the Spirit bears witness that we are children of God, justified by Him.

Through Jesus, we have received precious faith—a gift from God, rooted in His righteousness (2 Peter 1:1). This faith is not static or passive; it is meant to grow and be nurtured. As we walk with Christ, we are empowered by His grace to live lives of godliness. In 2 Peter 1:5-8, we are encouraged to nourish our faith with virtues such as moral excellence, knowledge, self-control, perseverance, godliness, brotherly affection, and love. As we grow in these qualities, our faith becomes more vibrant and fruitful. The more we reflect these attributes, the more we become like Christ, and the more we experience the power of His presence in our lives. Without these qualities, however, we risk becoming spiritually blind—alive but unable to fully see the depths of God's will for us.

Verse 10 of 2 Peter calls us to diligently "confirm our calling and election". While our life in Christ begins with faith, it must grow and manifest in action.

Faith, when supplemented with godly virtues, grows, and is transformed, aligning our hearts and minds with God's will.

The Christian life is not just about believing, but about growing, transforming, and living out the truths of the gospel in every area of life. Ultimately it is impossible without the help of the Holy Spirit. As I have personally discovered, we cannot live as Christ intends without His presence and power. The good news is, we are invited to ask. In Matthew 7:7, Jesus promises, "Ask, and you will receive." God is eager to give us the strength, wisdom, and grace we need to live in a way that honours Him.

Meditate

What comes to your mind when thinking about your Decisions and Desires after today's study? Meditate and add anything that comes to your mind to the prayer list below.

Time to Pray:

- Thank you, Heavenly Father, for Your everlasting and limitless love. Thank You for making me Yours again and sending Your Son Jesus to die on the cross for me, to save me from my sins and eternal death. Thank You for salvation and thank You for Your Holy Spirit. I worship You and surrender my whole life and being to You and Your will.

- Lord, You say in Your word that You will give wisdom to those who ask, so I ask for wisdom and revelation that gives me a deep, personal intimate insight into the true knowledge of God.
- I ask You to open the eyes of my heart, that it may be enlightened. I pray You'll flood my eyes with Your light by the Holy Spirit so that I will know and cherish the hope that You O God have set before me, as Your own.
- I pray that I will begin to know the exceeding, immeasurable, unlimited, and surpassing greatness of Your active power in me as I believe in You.
- This is in accordance with the mighty power that raised Jesus from the dead, that gave Him all authority and appointed Him as Head of the Church in which He fills, protects, and keeps me as His body (bride).
- May grace and peace be multiplied to me in the knowledge of You and Jesus my Lord. In Jesus' name, Amen.

"As a face is reflected
in water, so the heart
reflects the real person."
Proverbs 27:19

(Source: www.biblehub.com)

“I See and Feel Your Love”

Day 14

Reading of the Day: Matthew 14

In verse 13 of today's scripture, we read that when Jesus heard what happened to John the Baptist, He left where He was by boat to go to a deserted place to be by Himself. We can assume He was troubled and sad with the news He had just heard. I would like to use this as an example to encourage you. Sometimes it is ok to take time to yourself to think and process your emotions, away from the crowds, noise, and other voices. Time alone can sometimes be all the healing you need, to gather your strength and thoughts to reset. Jesus' followers heard He had left, and they decided to follow Him. This could be because they wanted more teachings, or they could see He was hurting and wanted to comfort Him and not leave Him alone. We will not know the actual reason but let's try to imagine the different possibilities. They loved Jesus and followed Him wherever He went, the scriptures say that most of them travelled by foot (remember in this story Jesus travelled to this specific deserted place by boat and so this would have been an exceptionally long walking journey). This shows that as people, we have the ability to be there for each other, go the extra mile to check on others, comfort them and even bless them with our presence. Humanity is to be united; we are not supposed to leave each other alone or isolate ourselves all the time but be concerned and intentional with other hearts and experiences.

Furthermore, verse 14 tells us that Jesus saw them, and He was moved by compassion for them and healed their sicknesses. Someone that has true love can recognise love, receive love, accept the love, and give love back. That's shown here as Jesus saw their care and concern for Him in that moment. I personally do not think they were there for their own gain but that they were there for Jesus and showed:

- Humility - they didn't think about themselves but wanted to put Jesus' needs first.
- Selflessness - they walked a long way to be there for Jesus.

In Jesus' pain and sadness with the news He just heard, He saw their care. This could have lifted His Spirit and made Him want to respond to their kindness with His love and compassion. He did not turn them away requesting to be left alone but he stepped out of His own emotions, saw them, had compassion, and then healed them. Now that is love.

This story demonstrates God's everlasting showing love in many ways. And because of this, He wants us to love others in this way by being intentional, compassionate, empathetic, and thoughtful. Loving others can look different in every circumstance. Sometimes it is to give people a hug then leave them alone for a short while or sometimes it's being present and speaking with them. Whatever it is, lead with love and if you are ever unsure on how to love in a particular moment or if it feels difficult to love, ask God to help you and speak to you. Afterall, God is love and He is our Father and our helper.

Meditate

What comes to your mind when thinking about your Decisions and Desires after today's study? Meditate and add anything that comes to your mind to the prayer list below.

Time to Pray:

- Thank you, God, for Your everlasting and unconditional love, healing, and compassion for us always.
- I pray to be surrounded by Godly, truthful, and kind people.
- I pray that you will transform me into a compassionate, sincere, and loving person that is intentional, empathetic, thoughtful and does not expect anything in return.
- I pray to be appreciative, thankful and have a heart of gratitude always.

- Lord forgive and protect me from the sins of the heart - pride, selfishness, greed, unforgiveness, self-centeredness and unhealthy self-isolation.
- When I'm feeling down and sad, lead me to a fruitful place in You. Do not let me isolate myself where no one can help me or where I cannot find You due to my own decisions.

Scripture to Meditate on:

"Come to me, all who labour and are heavy laden, and I will give you rest" (Matthew 11:28).

"So do not fear, for I am with you; do not be dismayed, for I am your God. I will strengthen you and help you; I will uphold you with my righteous right hand" (Isaiah 41:10).

"And so we know and rely on the love God has for us. God is love. Whoever lives in love lives in God, and God in them." 1 John 4:16.

"Love the Lord your God with all your heart and with all your soul and with all your mind and with all your strength.' The second is this: 'Love your neighbour as yourself.' There is no commandment greater than these" (Mark 12:30-31).

(Source: www.biblehub.com)

"If any of you lacks
wisdom, let him ask God,
who gives generously to
all without reproach, and
it will be given him."
James 1:5

(Source: www.biblehub.com)

"I Look Good... Don't I?"

Day 15

Reading of the Day: 1 Peter 3:3-6.

We are called to let our beauty not only be external but most importantly internal. Our inner person, our heart, soul, and mind should be full of love, beauty, and gentleness; so that we have sincere and pure hearts that reflect the love of Christ. Though the word beauty is often feminised, we must know and respond to the fact that God wants all of us to be focused on beautifying our hearts and souls whether we are female or male. This is particularly important because we must remember whatever is dwelling or growing inside of us, will always eventually come out (good or bad) and may not always allow us to fulfil the will of God in our lives. We see this all over scripture, such as:

- *"As a face is reflected in water, so the heart reflects the real person" (Proverbs 27:19).*
- *"The tongue can bring death or life; those who love to talk will reap the consequences" (Proverbs 18:21).*
- *"But the Lord said to Samuel, "Do not look at his appearance or at the height of his stature, because I have rejected him; for God sees not as man sees, for man looks at the outward appearance, but the Lord looks at the heart" (1 Samuel 16:7).*
- *"You blind Pharisee, first clean the inside of the cup and of the dish, so that the outside of it may become clean*

also.... So you, too, outwardly appear righteous to men, but inwardly you are full of hypocrisy and lawlessness" (Matthew 23:26 & 28).

- *"These people honour me with their lips, but their hearts are far from me" (Matthew 15:8).*
- *"Above all else, guard your heart, for everything you do flows from it" (Proverbs 4:23).*

(Source: www.biblehub.com)

Reflecting on the scriptures above, I really want God to work on me from the inside. I personally do not want to look only good on the outside but be a horrible person or allow things like unforgiveness, pride or jealousy to live within me. As God's children, we should be desiring God in us all the time and this is what God promises us. Jesus said "Remain in Me, and I will remain in you. For a branch cannot produce fruit if it is severed from the vine, and you cannot be fruitful unless you remain in Me" (John 15:4). Therefore, as Christ lives in us, He changes us from the inside out. 2 Corinthians 5:17 reads "Therefore if anyone is in Christ, he is a new creature; the old things passed away; behold, all things have become new." This is so that we can be fully renewed and transformed as children of God. We can simultaneously live in a broken world yet still be whole and loving while drawing others to Christ. It is vital to be transformed and changed by God, and to not allow yourself to think 'oh I'm fine and I'm a good person' or settle at 'this is just the way I am.' Only God is good and perfect, but he works for us to enable us to become perfect in Him. Certain life experiences, upbringings and the ways and culture of the world have a way of shaping us internally impacting our behaviours, decisions, desires, and personality. But the Bible lets us know that although they are all influences, we have the power to control the decisions we make going forward. We also see this throughout the Bible:

- *"Don't copy the behaviour and customs of this world, but let God transform you into a new person by changing the way you think. Then you will learn to know God's will for you, which is good and pleasing and perfect" (Romans 12:2).*
- *"You are the salt of the earth. But what good is salt if it has lost its flavour? Can you make it salty again? It will be thrown out and trampled underfoot as worthless" (Matthew 5:13).*
- *"…let your light shine before others, that they may see your good deeds and glorify your Father in heaven" (Matthew 5:16).*

  (Source: www.biblehub.com)

We can only fulfil this and undo the works of the world and negative life experiences by asking and allowing God to change, heal and strengthen us, and to also change the way we think and feel. This may require Him removing any stubbornness, pride, or laziness within us, in order to fill our hearts so we can love what He loves and hate what He hates.

Here are some ways God can work on the inside of us and cultivate His work:

- Through Prayer. Prayer changes all things as it is a way of communicating with God. It can speak to every area of our lives if we submit this to God.
- Through Worship. Worship is a spiritual discipline we must cultivate as it gives God all the glory and honour in our lives. It is an act of obedience and gratitude to God which not just comes from our mouth but through the way we live. It turns our focus and attention to Him and helps us to remember that He is sovereign, so we are to be obedient to Him and what He requires of us. It changes our positioning and humbles us to be open for transformation.
- Through Bible Study. Reading, studying, and mediating the word of God changes us because it IS God's word. Hebrews 4:12 says "For the word of God is alive and powerful. It is sharper than the sharpest two-edged sword, cutting

between soul and spirit, between joint and marrow. It exposes our innermost thoughts and desires." God touches our minds as we study His word. This includes the way we think, imagine and reason, so we can become more like Him.

- By surrounding yourself with people that cultivate God's change in you to be better and more like Him (see Psalm 1:1). Sometimes we can be around people that can give us the wrong advice and who influence us to do things we should not be doing. This is why prayer is particularly important, because God will reveal to you who you're around and who you should or should not confide in.
- Learning to take correction and feedback from people who know you and love you. We all have 'blind spots' (areas about ourselves that we cannot see) so when we are corrected in love by others, this helps us to see ourselves from a different perspective and look at how we can become better.
- By trying new things that push you out of our comfort zone. Trust that God is always with you so when you step out of what is comfortable you can overcome fear and start to learn new things

about yourself. You may even discover some new gifts, talents, and strengths, like Esther, Moses and Gideon did in the Bible. God knew what was inside of them and what they needed to become to fulfil His plans, all they needed to do was to step out in faith in obedience. And as a result, they fulfilled their individual purposes in unbelievable ways. Remember God is "able to do far more abundantly than all that we ask or think, according to the power at work within us" (Ephesians 3:20), that's God's power in US!

Therefore, give your heart and entire being to God and He will change you every day to become more like Him, to have a heart and mind like Him, and to fulfil His will so your life can give Him the glory. So, we can then say like Apostle Paul: "I have been crucified with Christ and I no longer live, but Christ lives in me. The life I now live in the body, I live by faith in the Son of God, who loved me and gave Himself for me" (Galatians 2:20).

Further Scriptures to Meditate on:

"The LORD your God will circumcise your hearts and the hearts of your descendants, so that you may love Him with all your heart and with all your soul, and live" (Deuteronomy 30:6).

"This is the covenant I will make with the people of Israel after that time" declares the LORD. "I will put my law in their minds and write it on their hearts. I will be their God, and they will be My people" (Jeremiah 31:33).

"Yet you, LORD, are our Father. We are the clay, You are the potter; we are all the work of Your hand" (Isaiah 64:8).

(Source: www.biblehub.com)

Meditate

What comes to your mind when thinking about your Decisions and Desires after today's study? Meditate and add anything that comes to your mind to the prayer list below.

Time to pray:

- Thank You God for salvation and that You now live and move inside of me.
- I ask for forgiveness in any way I have focused solely on the external, or when I have been wise in my own eyes and proudful, thinking I know it all. Also, for those times I have thought less of myself, undermining your love for me and who You have called me to be.

- I ask You Father to come into my life, mind, heart, body, and soul so You can take Your rightful place. Remove all the sin, pain and trauma and any other darkness that life or the world has thrown at me. God, please heal and restore me with Your love, strength, and power.
- Build and change me to be more like You, fulfilling my purpose and destiny that includes loving myself and others, and drawing others to God.
- Help me to have the right people around me on this journey of life and remove anyone that causes me to be the opposite of what You want. Fill me with Your power and confidence to try new things and not be overwhelmed with fear.
- I pray to become disciplined spiritually through prayer, worship, Bible study and serving You always. Thank You for forgiveness and grace. In Jesus' name, Amen.

Further Scriptures to Meditate on:

"And I am certain that God, who began the good work within you, will continue His work until it is finally finished on the day when Christ Jesus returns" (Philippians 1:6).

(Source: www.biblehub.com)

“Whom have I in heaven
but you? And there is
nothing on earth that I
desire besides you.”
Psalm 73:25

(Source: www.biblehub.com)

“When Was the Last Time I Prayed?”

Day 16

Prayer is a means to communicate with God and is vital to our spiritual growth and daily lives as Christ followers and as God's children. To build healthy relationships in general life, it requires communication on a deeper level and that's what prayer is for us and God. We have the means to speak to God about everything, and at any time. We see many examples in the Bible of the different types of prayers but at its core, prayer cements our relationship with God through vulnerability and telling Him everything. But sometimes in life we can go through moments where we don't feel like praying or we genuinely feel like we can't pray and talk to God. But this is not helpful nor good for us, we'll most likely see the effects over time as it affects the way we think, feel, treat others and what we begin to desire. In order to keep growing we must overcome this sin quickly (see how Samuel views this in 1 Samuel 12:23).

Here are some causes prayerlessness:

- Unbelief
- Fear
- Doubt
- Disappointment and discouragement
- Sin and guilt
- Laziness and not being disciplined
- Busyness and distractions
- Pride

All of these can distort our view and understanding of who God is, who He says we are and what He calls us to do. This is what sin does. Therefore, the importance of why we need to pray is even more important. We need God to intervene in the world around us and in our lives, so prayer is not only a requirement but an invitation for God to have dominion and His will to be done. Prayer is more for us than it is for God. It is important to humble ourselves before God, knowing we have no control, wisdom, or strength without Him. Otherwise, certain areas of our lives can be available to the devil to destroy our faith. Every day when we wake up, we may face new challenges but it's also an opportunity to fulfil God's will on earth. How will we know what to do or what we need if we do not seek God and put all areas of our life under the authority of God? With the faith that God will lead, protect, and provide for us. Prayer opens and closes doors that we can never do on our own (2 Chronicles 7:14).

In Luke 18:1, just before telling one of His parables Jesus said that *"...men ought always to pray, and not to faint."* He proceeded to tell the parable and described a widow that kept approaching a judge to ask for justice, and she never gave up. She was very persistent and kept coming to him, even though he kept refusing. But after a while the judge thought to Himself that even though he doesn't fear God or people, it would be a good idea for him to grant the widow her desire so that she would not come and attack him (which shows what kind of heart he had!). Jesus reflected on this and said, "Listen to what the unjust judge says. And will not God bring about justice for His chosen ones, who cry out to Him day and night? Will he keep putting them off? I tell you; He will see that they get justice, and quickly. However, when the Son of Man comes, will he find faith on the earth?" (Luke 18:6-8). God hears everything. Whether it is when we pray aloud, whisper to ourselves, think it in our minds or our hearts or within a conversation. And He always answers. Now the answer might not be what we want or think we should hear e.g. it might be a 'no' or 'not yet'. He may tell you that 'you need to become more patient' or 'you need to forgive that person, so your heart is free to receive.' But we have to remember that God is good, meaning there are no evil or bad intentions in Him and so we have the freedom to trust in every answer He gives, even if the answer feels a little delayed. God loves us and wants the best for us which is in His will. Prayer enables us to ask for things but most importantly to become what God has created us to be. Through conversations with God, through the yes's and no's, God leads us on the right path of our lives and does not allow us to just be doing our own thing outside of His will. Here are some thoughts on why it is important to pray:

- It gives God all the glory. It increases and encourages our full reliance on God because He is the all-knowing, omnipotent God that hears and answers our prayers. It helps us to know God more and experience His grace, love, and mercy. See 2 Corinthians 12:8-9 and Jeremiah 29:12-13.
- It helps us to receive His forgiveness and therefore to forgive others. See Luke 11:4.
- Jesus showed us what communion and relationship building looks like with God and that is prayer. See Mark 1:35-38. Prayer makes us develop a trusting and true relationship with God.
- We have the opportunity to ask God for things whether it is physical or spiritual, we are promised that He will give to us according to His will and word. See Matthew 7:11, John 16:24, and John 9:31.
- Keeps us on the path of holiness and righteousness, as we pray to overcome and discern all temptation. See Matthew 26:41.

- It ensures that God's will is being done in our lives and those around us. See Matthew 6:9-10.
- As we ask for power, discernment, wisdom, and strength, this protects us from the plans of the devil. Also destroys the work of the devil. See Luke 10:19 & Matthew 18:18-20.
- Keeps us humble and thankful. Allowing God to change, prune and mould us to how He originally created us. Taking away all the negative labels and experiences that try to shape us daily.

Now you know the benefits and importance of prayer, if you ever feel as though you don't want to pray, you must, (emphasis on the 'must') overcome that feeling in the name of Jesus. The devil knows the power of your prayer and wants to stop or reduce your faith, but you are more than a conqueror (Romans 8:37) and you have the strength of the Holy Spirit to keep going and pursuing God (Isaiah 40:31). Your deliverance, peace, direction, and faith are through your consistent prayer and communication with God. So as said perfectly by Apostle Paul, "Rejoice always, pray without ceasing, give thanks in all circumstances; for this is the will of God in Christ Jesus for you" (1 Thessalonians 5:16-17).

And so, I encourage you by saying; "Let us then approach God's throne of grace with confidence, so that we may receive mercy and find grace to help us in our time of need" (Hebrews 4:16).

Praying with confidence in this scripture means:

- Boldly
- Freely
- Constantly
- Without reservation
- Without fancy words (I don't have to show or present myself a certain way)
- Persistence
- Remembering that God's throne of grace is just and compassionate.

Meditate

What comes to your mind when thinking about your Decisions and Desires after today's study? Meditate and add anything that comes to your mind to the prayer list below.

Time to Pray

- Thank you, God, for the opportunity to commune and the ability to build my relationship with You through prayer.
- I ask for forgiveness for being disobedient, proud and for letting earthly things determine how

much I follow Your instructions to pray always. I ask for Your grace and mercy.

- You know what can cause me to become less prayerful, so I want to put it before You God now and pray for the strength and the power to overcome it. This could be fear, unbelief, laziness, busyness, doubt etc. None of these will work for it is written:
  "No weapon formed against you shall prosper, and every tongue which rises against you in judgement, you shall condemn." In the name of Jesus! (Isaiah 54:17).
  (Source: www.biblehub.com)
- I pray for the strength and zeal to study the word of God more, because the more I know You God, the more I will know about myself. (It enables you to quote scripture whilst praying as evidence to back up everything you say and helps you keep on praying God's will).

Search me, O God, and
know my heart! Try me
and know my thoughts!
And see if there be any
grievous way in me
and lead me in the way
everlasting!
Psalm 139:23-24

(Source: www.biblehub.com)

When Sitting At His Thone

Day 17

To be constant in prayer is to know why you are praying. There are many examples in the Bible as to why people pray and the types of prayers to pray.

There are many examples and stories within scripture detailing different individuals' prayers. One of these that we will focus on is Hannah's persistent requests to God.

Hannah sought God for the fruit of the womb. She wanted a child so asked God for one and made a vow that she'd give the child back to God to make sure it would give God glory. She also didn't give up in her prayers as she knew only God could help her. She prayed all the time even in anguish, suffering and pain. This shows us that God wants us to communicate with him no matter the emotion we are feeling, He can handle it. Even when we're lacking in faith or if we're feeling sad, tired and weak, prayer is even more important at this time.

Hannah prayed through her tears and God didn't ridicule her or tell her off. He hears and understands every single word or tear because we are His children. Maybe God gave Hannah a child after she made the vow. Could this be because she made it less about her? We have to check our motives when asking God for things. Over the years, she probably had varied reasons as to why she wanted a child. For example, it could have been to prove Peninnah (who was her husband's 2nd wife who already had children and had mocked Hannah for being childless) wrong? Or to keep her husband happy? Or to prove to others she was not barren? There could be many reasons, but it wasn't until she decided to sincerely pray to God for a child and surrender her child to God should He give her one, that she eventually became pregnant with Samuel. Now, I don't know if that's the reason why she finally got Samuel, but it's a point worth considering.

What are the motives behind what you are asking God for through prayer? I encourage you to ask the Holy Spirit to check them and reveal to you where you may have ill or skewed reasons. God is always ready to hear and answer our prayers, we learn in yesterday's devotional that with persistent prayer and faith God will answer us, just like He did for Hannah. So today, I encourage you to not lose your faith, whatever you are seeking God for and despite how long for, pray with persistence and belief and pure intentions. I trust that He will answer you according to His will, and not yours.

Further Scriptures to Meditate on:

- Philippians 4:6: *"Do not be anxious about anything, but in every situation, by prayer and petition, with thanksgiving, present your requests to God."*

- Hebrews 11:6: *"And without faith it is impossible to please God, because anyone who comes to him must believe that he exists and that he rewards those who earnestly seek him"*.
- James 4:3: reads *"When you ask, you do not receive, because you ask with the wrong motives, that you may spend it on your selfish desires/indulgences,"* but this isn't just money related. It can also relate to pride, haughtiness, revenge, anger, unforgiveness, selfishness etc - things that do not last.
  (Source: www.biblehub.com)

Meditate

What comes to your mind when thinking about your Decisions and Desires after today's study? Meditate and add anything that comes to your mind to the prayer list below.

Time to pray:

- Father God, please assess my motives and show me where my motives are self-centred and not about giving You the glory.
- I ask You to reveal within me if I have any wrong or selfish motives in my heart and help me to

have a sincere and humble heart. Help me to commune with You out of obedience and love.

- I pray my faith will not fail, that I will earnestly always seek you, trusting that your timing and provision is perfect for me.

“But seek first the kingdom
of God and his righteousness,
and all these things will be
added to you.”
Matthew 6:33

(Source: www.biblehub.com)

"I Made It Through!"

Day 18

Reading of the Day: James 1:4 & John 18.

Jesus tells us that in our lives, we will go through various trials and challenges (John 16:33) that ultimately test and refine our faith (John 16:33). But when we go through these trials, I don't know about you, but it can sometimes feel really difficult to understand how to respond and remain strong. But the Bible gives us guidance through God's promises and the fruits of the Holy Spirit to help us. Patience is one of these fruits. The Greek word for patience in Greek is 'Hupomone' which means endurance, steadfastness, and constancy. Before learning this definition, I used to interpret it meaning waiting and sitting or being passive. So, if we were to expand the James 1:4 verse of the day using this definition, it would say something like 'let endurance, steadfastness and constancy have its perfect work in you; that you may be perfect and complete, lacking nothing.'

This means we are not to be swayed, discouraged or inconsistent but to grow in our ability to endure things, learn to wait things out despite what we are going through, in other words, to keep pushing through. How can we become more patient? By being in situations that require patience from us. This could be finishing a challenging task at work, having a family member that has an unkind way of speaking or treating others but is on a journey to change or by facing financial or health challenges. It's important to understand that we can only grow through what we go through. Patience helps us to get through life challenges by allowing us to make sound decisions, enabling us to have a clearer vision on what is going on around and within us. And so, I would encourage you, when you are going through challenges seek God and ask Him to show you what areas of your life He is working on and changing for the better.

It is very typical for us to face trials with fear and unbelief, but this only produces bitterness, sin, worry and further unbelief, and even pushes us to start listening to the wrong advice. It is also typical for us to become unbelieving when under affliction, but we have to remember that unbelieving and doubting God draws us away from God. Going through tough times can also make us rush to find solutions but trying to escape the trials through our own means and wisdom in an ill way can also be a sin. That is why we should always be prayerful and aim to lean on God. Remember the Lord's prayer in Matthew 6:9-13? Jesus encourages us to say, *'Lord lead us not into temptation,'* because trials can tempt us to sin, even just by what we say in moments of distress (remember life and death are in the power of the tongue). We need to be neutralised by God's abundant grace, through prayer and having the patience to hear from Him in this moment and comforted by His promises in the Bible. Looking back at trials retrospectively builds our faith as we see God's wonder at work, and we start to understand the reason for a trial which only draws us closer to God.

The Crucifixion of Jesus is a life trial I would like to pay some attention to provide a unique perspective to help us with the way we respond to trials and challenges. Firstly, we see in today's reading (John 18), that Jesus knows all things and He knew what was about to happen to Him. He was prepared and remained calm when Judas and the soldiers approached Him (John 18:4) although it was not an easy task that He was about to embark on. There's something powerful about knowing what is to come but even more powerful in knowing that you can persevere by resting in the God who knows your beginning and your end, the God who has all power and authority in all creation and is faithful to protect and deliver us as we journey throughout life. And so, it is so important to trust God during the trials we face in life. I know this sounds easier said than done but only if we think we can do this in our strength. He'll provide the right people, the strength, insight, wisdom, vision and discernment we need at the right time, without these things we will respond in the wrong way. For example, we see in John 18:10, Simon Peter responds to Judas and the soldiers in anger by rushing out and cutting off the high priest's servant's ear. That was not supposed to be the right response. Why? Because he didn't have discernment of God's plan and timing. That's why Jesus said to him in verse 11 "shall I not drink the cup which my Father has given me?"

There are some familiar Christian songs we sing that include lyrics such as 'fill my cup Lord and make me whole.' But in reality, to be filled up means that we have to go through things that will empty out any negativity in us first, this process does not always feel good. But because our Father is good, we know it is to fill us with more of Him and His goodness and more so, it is for the Kingdom and for His glory. If the high Priests' servants did not take Jesus, then we would not be saved today (or perhaps it may have happened another way.) So, while the cup for Jesus to drink from was hard and difficult, it was required as part of God's plan. Jesus already knew what was to happen, that's why He was patient in the storm and was even able to pray just beforehand, asking for not His will but God's will be done (Matthew 26:36-39).

We know God is a very present help in our troubles and victory always belongs to Jesus. So, through everything we can be bold and confident knowing that weeping may endure for the night, but joy comes in the morning.

Also, Jesus specifically said *"My Father"* in (John 18:11). This reminds us that through every trial, God's position as Father in our lives will never change. And so, we are to remember our own identity in God as His children. He will save us, guide us, protect us, and teach us as we would expect from an earthly father. We can hold on to His promise that His plans for us are to give us life, hope, and a good future (Jeremiah 29:11) and there is purpose and an end date to every trial we experience.

Meditate

What comes to your mind when thinking about your Decisions and Desires after today's study? Meditate and add anything that comes to your mind to the prayer list below.

Time to Pray:

- Thank you, Father, for who you are and thank you for your everlasting love, mercy, and grace.
- Thank you, Father, for Your Kingdom, salvation and redeeming me back to you.

- Thank you, Father, that in all things, everything works together for my good and that because You are Victorious, I am victorious.
- Father, I ask for forgiveness for not having faith at times and not trusting in You. I ask for You to forgive me for the times I've been seeking to escape trials through lies; where I have been deceitful; where I have had pride and unbelief or where I have complained and murmured.
- I pray to grow spiritually to see what is to come, to be prepared, and watchful, and be on guard ensuring I do not fall into slumber.
- I pray to have understanding and to be ready to respond in faith with the strength to endure all things. May Your will be done always.
- May I not stand in the way of Your will but be Kingdom minded and focused.
- I pray that I will be surrounded with the right people who can give me sound advice, not to influence me to follow a wrong path in life.
- I ask for the grace to be patient and to steadfastly endure through every situation.

Thank you, Father, in Jesus' name. Amen.

"And we know that for
those who love God all
things work together for
good, for those who are
called according to his
purpose."
Romans 8:28

(Source: www.biblehub.com)

“Bread and Milk Are Both Good For You”

Day 19

Reading of the Day: Joshua 1:8.

In today's scripture, God was talking to Joshua when He told him to continue the work of Moses after he died. The instruction God gave to Joshua, can also be an instruction for us to in our daily lives:

Not allow God's word to depart from us but instead be intentional in meditating on and speaking God's word. We are encouraged to hold the word close to our hearts and cherish it, not to handle it carelessly.

To meditate is for us to consistently reflect on and consider what God is telling us through the various stories, letters, poems, and prophecies in the Bible. Hebrews 4:12 describes the Bible a 'living word' which means it is alive and active, consistently speaking to us at any point in time. As it is breathed by the same Holy Spirit in us, it will forever be relevant to our lives to today, 2 Timothy 3:16 puts it best "All Scripture is inspired by God and is useful to teach us what is true and to make us realise what is wrong in our lives. It corrects us when we are wrong and teaches us to do what is right."

When you meditate on something all the time you'll eventually become like that thing. It starts to change the way you think, speak, and even live. So, when the Bible says we should meditate on God's word so that we will do according to all that is written; it means we will become who God has called us to be and live righteous in His will. Sometimes we think we have the ability to change ourselves, or say "when I change, I will do xyz" but the truth is we can't change ourselves, it is only God and His word that changes and moulds us. Therefore, our decisions and desires will more easily adhere to all that is written in the Bible.

1 Peter 2:2 tells us "Like newborn babies, crave pure spiritual milk, so that by it you may grow up in your salvation", We need to get to a place where we know that without it we will stunt our spiritual growth and can become empty and we are able to discern if this is happening. Like a baby would cry out when they are hungry for more milk, so we should be able to cry out to God through seeking Him to be filled and sustained. The Bible also likens God's word to 'bread' as it sustains us, feeds us, and gives us the right spiritual nutrients we need to be healthy and effective just like with natural food for our bodies. As all of God's word is perfect, I would encourage you to believe in all of it, and not pick and choose what parts you want to obey. It has to be all that is written in it but if there is any area that you do not understand and need more clarity on firstly ask the Holy Spirit and speak to your church leaders and Christian friends for help you.

I'm excited for you to begin and/or continue studying the word of God.

Meditate

What comes to your mind when thinking about your Decisions and Desires after today's study? Meditate and add anything that comes to your mind to the prayer list below.

Time to pray:

- Thank you, God, for Your word that always gives me access to You, Your thoughts, and Your righteousness.
- I pray for strength to prioritise and be consistent in studying the Bible.
- I ask for power and strength to take control of my thoughts and any distractions so that I will meditate and consider Your word.
- I pray for obedience to do what is right (sometimes we can know the truth or the right decision to make but still choose not to for many reasons e.g. fear, peer pressure, lack of self-control, unforgiveness).
- I pray to desire Your word consistently and be not lazy to pursue it. I pray over my desires, willingness, passion, and intentionality and submit them to your will.

"Casting all your anxieties on him, because he cares for you."
1 Peter 5:7

(Source: www.biblehub.com)

“Stronger Than I’ve Ever Been”

Day 20

Reading of the Day: 1 Samuel 30.

We can only be empowered and draw our strength from God through consistently developing our relationship with Him. The power of God's boundless might is the unlimited force of His strength that we freely have access to. Therefore, we are encouraged to not lean on ourselves, relying on our own strength but begin to look to God.

So how can we be strong in the Lord?

- By putting on the full armour of God
- Knowing who God is and who you are in Christ
- Knowing all God has done for you

To be able to have the armour of God and use it correctly, we have to be strong IN God (so strong in our belief, faith, reliance, and trust in God). 1 Samuel 30 is a perfect example of what being strong in the Lord looks like, we see in verses 3-6 that David was distressed because he had just come back from war and saw that the Amalekites had burned his town, taken captive all the residents including all the children and wives. The people he was with cried until there was no more strength in them and his men began to turn their anger toward Him and wanted to stone him because of the bitterness they were feeling. Through David's tears we can assume this would have been hard for David as a leader to witness and experience and must have completely discouraged him. If we put ourselves in this situation, how would we feel and respond? You may have wanted to go into complete hiding, felt that you had failed or that you were completely alone.

However, despite the fact David was going through a time of confusion, attack, disappointment, fear and not knowing what to do next as a leader, 1 Samuel 30:6 tells us "But David found strength in the Lord his God". In my opinion, this is an extremely profound and powerful response in this story. This is because David was completely aware of his feelings, but he didn't let that drive his decisions. Being strong in the Lord is knowing God and who you are as God's child. He remembered that God is his mighty warrior, his defender, his hope, and his shepherd so he trusted that God would help him and provide for his needs at this moment in time. The might of God does not work if we sit passively, His might only works if we rely on it, step out, and do the work. This is exemplified when David asked God what he should do and if he would succeed, God responded to him saying "Yes, go after them. You will surely recover everything that was taken from you!" (verse 6). You see, all David needed was the strength to go to God, God then gave David complete strength by letting him know he was with him and heard his cry, answering his question by giving guidance and importantly giving David the confidence of what is going to happen (God said 'you will surely'). With the strength received from God, David was able to rise leading his men and recovered everything the Amalekites had taken, including his two wives" (verse 19).

Trusting and walking with God is not having an attitude of:

- 'I do all I can, and God helps me with what I cannot do or the rest' or
- 'I do nothing, and God does everything' nor is it
- 'I do everything, and God does nothing.'

It is about us working with God, seeking His will, relying on, and trusting his promises, just as David did. It is about having the faith that God is in control, will lead you and you following through despite what you may feel or see physically. Following God renews our strength in God to do what we need to do on earth, whether that is in our careers, families, or health for example. Isaiah 40:31 contains a great promise of strength for anyone that may be feeling weary (like how David was feeling at the start of this story). The scripture says "they who wait for the Lord shall renew their strength; they shall mount up with wings like eagles; they shall run and not be weary; they shall walk and not faint."

Meditate

What comes to your mind when thinking about your Decisions and Desires after today's study? Meditate and add anything that comes to your mind to the prayer list below.

Time to Pray:

- Heavenly Father teach me how to partner with and rely on You so that I can be strong in You wherever I go, in whatever I do.
- May I not grow weary in everything that I am doing, but may I keep my head up today and experience your strength, confidence, and guidance today.
- Thank you that you are the strength of my life, In Jesus' name, Amen.

“I have stored up your
word in my heart, that I
might not sin against you.”
Psalm 119:11

(Source: www.biblehub.com)

“It’s The Perfect Amount”

Day 21

Reading of the Day: Exodus 16.

In verse 2 of today's scripture, we learn that when the Israelites were in the wilderness, they grew unhappy about the food Moses and Aaron was providing. They hungered for food to the extent they wished they would die by the hand of God in Egypt like the Egyptians did, comparing their lives to when they were in Egypt enjoying surplus food, they "sat around pots of meat and ate all the food" (verse 3). The reading of today brings to light many themes around God's provision, prayer, and greed.

Firstly, after God had delivered the Israelites from captivity, we see that they had verbally wished death upon themselves because they were not enjoying life like the benefits they perceived they experienced whilst being slaves. Their desires made them forgetful and thwarted their perception of what God had done for them and where they were in their journey to freedom. Sometimes we can fall victim to this, we can become shortsighted on the journey God has us on because of an urgent need we have or impatience to see God's blessings. We then start to speak in accordance with that negative feeling which ultimately can destroy our faith in the decisions we make, leading us away from God. The Bible says, "The tongue can bring death or life; those who love to talk will reap the consequences," and so it's important to be careful in what you say or desire when you're hungry, thirsty, in a wilderness or waiting season. Don't let it get you to a mental place of ungratefulness or forgetting where God has taken you from! This emotion or state of being can blind you from where you're going, just like it did to the Israelites, and it will please the enemy which is what we do not want. The best thing to do is to tell God how you are feeling and ask Him to help you work through those emotions because we know they are not permanent or rooted in truth.

Following the Israelites' complaints, we see God respond through Moses saying *"Behold, I will rain bread from heaven for you"* which reminds us that God hears everything - even the complaints that aren't even spoken to Him directly, he is in all our conversations (verse 8). So be encouraged by the fact that whenever you speak to God, He hears you (Isaiah 65:24). Don't ever worry or doubt that God hears your prayers, your questions and your worries. Be comforted that our Father God is alive and ever present no matter what and He is a God who answers and responds. Sometimes we complain to others about life challenges instead of God. In our minds we may think when we are talking to others we are not actually talking to God, so we can technically say what we want. But can we really when God can hear everything? However regardless of all, verse 8 also shows God is so compassionate and His love provides even when we complain and don't ask. We also see this with Sarah in Genesis 18:12-15.

In verses 16 to 19 God gives specific instructions on how to share the manna amongst the camp, God wanted them all to take what is enough for them, nothing more or less. But we read that some people in the camp took more than was needed, against God's instruction and this resulted in negative consequences for them. It is important that we handle God's provision with care and mindfulness, sometimes God will give detailed instructions as with this story but no matter what we are to be generous, caring, not greedy and find ways that everyone can partake and benefit from God's blessings in your life. Another example is in Colossians 3:23-24, this says *"Whatever you do, work at it with all your heart, as working for the Lord, not for human masters"*, *(Source: www.biblehub.com)*

God has provided work for us (job, volunteering or business) but wants us to handle our work in a way that pleases Him. Think about the ways God has provided for you and consider if you are managing His provisions in a way that is pleasing to Him, if you are unsure or feel as though you could do better, seek God in prayer and ask Him to help you with wisdom and a loving and obedient heart.

Meditate

What comes to your mind when thinking about your Decisions and Desires after today's study? Meditate and add anything that comes to your mind to the prayer list below.

Time to Pray:

- Heavenly Father, I thank You that You are the God that always hears and answers my prayers. I thank You for always providing for me, even the times when I have not asked you directly. Thank you for your love and compassion towards me.
- Your word instructs me in Philippians 2:4 to "Do everything without complaining and arguing. So that no one can criticise" me. And so, I ask for forgiveness for the times when I have allowed my emotions to change my view of You. Forgive me for all the times I have complained and murmured against You and Your work in my life. I ask for the wisdom and grace to not

complain and murmur but to see life as You see it for me and those around me.

- Help me to be a good steward of all that You provide me with and change my decisions and desires to be full of love, generosity, selflessness, and obedience to You.
- I pray to be content in You and with Your provision with gratitude, not to be looking at what others have so I become discontented (Philippians 4:11-13).

Further Scriptures to Meditate on:

Hebrews 13:5-6 reads "Keep your life free from the love of money (fleshly pursuits), and be content with what you have, for He has said, "I will never leave you nor forsake you" So we can confidently say, "The Lord is my helper; I will not fear; what can man do to me?". (Source: www.biblehub.com).

“Do not let your adorning be external—the braiding of hair and the putting on of gold jewellery, or the clothing you wear— but let your adorning be the hidden person of the heart with the imperishable beauty of a gentle and quiet spirit, which in God’s sight is very precious.”
1 Peter 3:3-4

(Source: www.biblehub.com)

“It Wasn’t Me”

Day 22

Reading of the Day: Philippians 2:13.

Here is today's scripture in different Bible versions:

- *"For it is God who works in you both to will and to do for His good pleasure."* (NKJV)
- *"For God is working in you, giving you desire and the power to do what pleases Him."* (NLT)
- *"God who is effectively at work in you, both to will and to work (that is strengthened, energising and creating in you the longing and the ability to fulfil your purpose) for His good pleasure."* (Amplified)

  (Source: www.biblehub.com)

Sometimes in our walk with God, we can sometimes feel discouraged or we that just 'don't have it in us' to do right, follow God's direction or to keep going but today's scripture gives us the insight and confidence that it is really God that enables us to live a righteous and holy life. Personally, this gives me great comfort that God being gracious, understands my nature and fills me with what I need to continue to live for Him as long as I choose to continue to give myself to Him. If God is willing and does live in us as the scripture promises, what is there for us to do? Well, Jesus tells us in John 15:4 that if we remain in Him then He will remain in us, only then can today's scripture truly come to pass in our lives. Here are some ways we can remain in God:

- Cultivate and bring to full effect your salvation by standing firm in the truth of who God is and that you are now saved in Jesus Christ.
- Actively pursue spiritual maturity by praying, bible study, worship and fasting.
- By being careful to follow God's precepts and word.
- Critical self-evaluation using the word of God to avoid anything that might offend God or discredit the name of Christ.

The Lord enables us to walk in our purpose. He strengthens us to follow Him and to say no to temptation. God gives us all we need to live a fruitful life that pleases Him. And it is amazing that He is the one who enables us to do that. 1 Corinthians 12:3 tells us that, "No one who is speaking by that Spirit of God says, "Jesus be cursed (damned)" and no one can say, "Jesus is Lord", except by the Holy Spirit". We need the Holy Spirit to direct us, 'for those who are led by the Spirit of God are sons of God.' The Spirit of God leads us to a Holy life free from permanently stumbling or derailing.

He is actively speaking, changing, empowering, protecting, guiding, leading, pruning, training, and teaching us to be more like Him in His perfect design in ways that may or may not feel so good. But we must remember it is to His will and good pleasure despite our temporary feelings. Our father leads us as children of God, and we read in Psalms 66:9 that "He preserves our lives and keeps our feet from slipping". When you read the rest of Psalm 66, it shows us that in all seasons, trials throughout life give God glory as we are victorious in every situation as He is with us and in us. Be comforted that it is by God's grace that we have God living in us and we have all it takes to live in accordance with His will if we choose to stay close and do life with God.

Meditate

What comes to your mind when thinking about your Decisions and Desires after today's study? Meditate and add anything that comes to your mind to the prayer list below.

Time to Pray:

- Thank you, God, for loving me so much that You are willing and do dwell in me to make me better by changing, pruning, leading, and guiding me.
- Thank You for not giving up on me and for always being faithful.
- Lord help me to be obedient to You, to cultivate and mature my salvation. Show me the ways I

may be dormant, lazy, or unbelieving and work in me to be better.

- Holy Spirit help me to critically evaluate the ways I have been offending You or discrediting the name of Christ whether it's in my thoughts, the way I speak or what I believe. And forgive me Father, I am sorry.
- Lord, I pray You will continue to work in me both to will and for your good pleasure, lead me and keep my feet from slipping. Fill me with the desire and strength to do Your will daily and not rely on my own works, ideas, strength, plans, wisdom. It's all you God, I need you! Thank you, Father.

Further Scriptures to Meditate On:

"By his divine power, God has given us everything we need for living a godly life. We have received all of this by coming to know him, the one who called us to himself by means of his marvellous glory and excellence" 2 Peter 1:3

(Source: www.biblehub.com)

“Each one must give as he
has decided in his heart,
not reluctantly or under
compulsion, for God loves a
cheerful giver.”
2 Corinthians 9:7

(Source: www.biblehub.com)

“Just Like God”

Day 23

Reading of the Day: Philippians 2.

The Bible teaches us that it is important to esteem (honour, regard) others more than ourselves, and to look out for the interest of others. However, at times in our lives, we as humans have the tendency to have pride in ourselves (which can be conceited), and as a result seek things that feed our own pride and align with our own plans, passions, and desires. This then drives the intrinsic motivations and ambitions we have to make life decisions whether big or small. However, the Bible shows us that Jesus, God in the flesh, practised humility when He was on earth, "He made Himself of no reputation taking the form of a bondservant and coming in the likeness of men. He humbled Himself and became obedient to the point of death, even the death of the cross" (Verse 7-8).

We have Jesus as the perfect example and blueprint to learn how to put others before ourselves. Jesus became obedient meaning He humbled himself by putting other people first to serve, help and support before thinking of Himself, which aligns with the commandment about loving our neighbours. However, the difference with the people of Philippi Paul was referring to in today's scripture, was that the people *"all seek their own, not the things which are of Christ Jesus"* (Philippians 2:21) and that there was "no-one like-minded, who will sincerely care for your state" (verse 20). When we practise humility, we are able to be bondservants like Christ, it increases our compassion and love for others by helping us to see more of others' needs as we have decreased ourselves in our own eyes. However, pride blinds our ability to see others because it makes us so self-centred that we mostly focus on ourselves. Jesus Christ humbled Himself to do the Lord's work and then glorify Him while still on earth, so why not us too? The goal whilst on earth for us is to be Christlike but sometimes, if we are to be honest, we do things with selfish ambition. Deep down there's pride somewhere e.g. we may be looking at what we can get out of a situation or seeing how it can benefit us before choosing to get involved. Instead, we should approach all areas of our lives by asking God how we can be of service to others, expecting nothing in return, especially as we have been called to serve. It is simply our job as a response to God's love for us, so we can now give this love to others.

Being humble is part of working out our salvation with awe inspired fear and trembling (Philippians 2:12).

Meditate

What comes to your mind when thinking about your Decisions and Desires after today's study? Meditate and add anything that comes to your mind to the prayer list below.

Time to pray:

- Heavenly Father, I thank you for showing me how I am to love and treat others, thank you for your patience and grace as I live for you and live to be like you.
- I ask for forgiveness for being selfish, self-centred, being proud and for doing things out of selfish ambition. Lord, I ask of You to fill me with more of You, Your insight, discernment and strength to love. Please remove all fears and bad influences drawing me away from Godly living. I ask to be made whole in Christ Jesus.
- I ask for a heart of humility and to be consistently obedient in being humble. Fill my heart to be generous and Christlike that loves and lifts others up above myself so I can serve.
- I choose to respond to Your love by being intentional in finding opportunities to help, serve and support others without expecting things in return, through conceit or selfish ambition.

  In Jesus' name, Amen.

Meditate on what you want to be known for in life, does it represent or show the love of Christ? The characteristics and fruits of the Spirit are love, joy, peace, patience, kindness, goodness, faithfulness, gentleness, and self-control, which one of these is God showing you need to develop in?

"With my whole heart I seek you; let me not wander from your commandments!"
Psalm 119:10

(Source: www.biblehub.com)

“I’ve Got Joy”

Day 24

Reading of the Day: Habakkuk 3:18.

"Yet I will rejoice in the Lord, I will joy in the God of my salvation."

In the verses before verse 18, Habakkuk states that even if he has nothing in this life, he'll still rejoice in the Lord. He puts it like this:

- If the fig tree and there be no fruit on the vines (could represent no fruit of his labour)
- If the fields yield no food (could represent famine)
- If the flock is cut off from fold and there shall be no herd in the stalls (could represent loneliness and no provision for his livelihood).

Despite all of this, he chooses to still rejoice in God because God saved him, and He is his strength. Habakkuk says that God will make his feet like a 'deer's foot.' Deers are secure in any terrain they find themselves in and will always be confident wherever they travel because of how God has designed them. And so, with us, spiritually we also have the sure-footed reliance that whatever situation we are in, God is with us (Isaiah 43:2). God gives us the grace, strength, and courage we need to advance and move forward in every terrain and season. Habakkuk goes on to say: "He makes me walk on higher heights" meaning that God makes us walk above our situation, circumstance, and worries. We have the power and grace to rise above it and fix our eyes on Jesus, just like Peter could have done whilst walking on water, by looking at Jesus and not at the wind, storms, or waves of the sea. Only then was he able to walk towards Jesus on unstable ground (any terrain). We have to come to a place where we can only rest in God with joy if we have this reliance on God.

Sometimes it is good to be comforted or accept affirmations and encouragement from others. But as Habakkuk did, we have to get to a point in our faith journey where we can self-affirm, speak comfort and blessings to ourselves, based on the truth about God, we see this in verses 18-19. Despite everything, Habakkuk could pick himself up by relying on God only. This is one of the joys of our salvation: that we have God our Heavenly Father who is always with us. 2 Corinthians 4:6 reads "For it is the God who commanded light to shine out of darkness, who has shone in our hearts to give the light of the knowledge of the glory of God in the face of Jesus". How amazing is it that we have Jesus, the light of God living in us to see us through and overcome all types of darkness. Whether it is depression, guilt, sin, addictions, unforgiveness or trauma, whatever you have been battling with, God is shining His light on it, delivering, restoring, and healing you every step of the way. I encourage you to trust Him, learn to lean on Him as Habakkuk habitually did and then you can enjoy the joys of your salvation in Jesus Christ. Be reminded that God always gets the glory. His gift of salvation means that He loves us and so we may be pressed on every side but not crushed because of Jesus, so we cannot lose heart.

Meditate:

What comes to your mind when thinking about your Decisions and Desires after today's study? Meditate and add anything that comes to your mind to the prayer list below.

Time to Pray:

- Thank you, God, for your love, peace, and protection.
- Lord help me to know how to speak comfort to myself using Your word, instead of always relying on others to comfort me.
- Forgive me for not seeing You as my comforter. I ask You to teach me how to turn to You always, even when it feels easier to talk to someone else. As You have promised, please comfort my spirit,

mind, and soul when I am sad or uncomfortable and lead me into Your life.

Scripture to Meditate on:

"We are pressed on every side by troubles, but we are not crushed. We are perplexed, but not driven to despair. We are hunted down, but never abandoned by God. We get knocked down, but we are not destroyed.

"That is why we never give up. Though our bodies are dying, our spirits are being renewed every day. For our present troubles are small and won't last very long. Yet they produce for us a glory that vastly outweighs them and will last forever! So, we don't look at the troubles we can see now; rather, we fix our gaze on things that cannot be seen. For the things we see now will soon be gone, but the things we cannot see will last forever." (2 Corinthians 4:8-10 & 16-18).

(Source: www.biblehub.com)

“As for that in the good soil, they are those who, hearing the word, hold it fast in an honest and good heart, and bear fruit with patience.”
Luke 8:15

(Source: www.biblehub.com)

"Only If..."

Day 25

Reading of the Day: Philippians 4.

Verse 4 in today's scripture instructs us to "Rejoice in the Lord always, Again I will say rejoice." Further through the chapter, in verse 8 Paul tells us one of the ways we can rejoice in the Lord, he says "We should think on good things but specifically if there's anything praiseworthy meditate on these things".

The key word that stood out to me personally, is 'if.' In dark and challenging times, the ability to consider the 'if's' can be difficult to do or even imagine that there may be a positive perspective or alternative outcome to what may be going on for us. But the Bible tells us to carefully search out that 'if' and then praise God. The positive praiseworthy thing could be anything, for example you may be learning a lesson about someone's character or being thankful that you're still alive after that accident or maybe it was an opportunity to get to know yourself better. These are the things that are praiseworthy. The Bible consistently reminds us that there is always light in what may seem/have seemed like a dark situation, for example in Psalms 30:5 it says, "weeping may endure for a night, but joy comes in the morning". And Romans 8:28 reminds us that "God causes everything to work together for the good of those who love God and are called according to his purpose for them.", this alone encourages us to search out what that 'good' is, through the Holy Spirit working on our perceptions and perspectives.

The Holy Spirit will provide you with the opportunity to meditate on the praiseworthy things, as that will strengthen your faith to keep going, the aim is not to be overcome but to be an overcomer. Verse 11 in today's scripture states "…I have learned in whatever state, I am to be content", why or how was Paul able to do this? Well Paul answers this question in verse 19, showing us his faith in God, "And my God shall supply all your needs according to His riches in glory by Christ Jesus". He also said, "I can do all things through Christ who strengthens me." Paul was so sure that whatever situation, circumstance or season he was in, he knew God and that's all he needed to be content. Being content is knowing who God is, realising that we cannot rely on ourselves and being ok with that. Otherwise, we'd be exhausted, have never ending desires and in a consistent state of frustration.

God will answer and provide all we need in an amazing way. Our needs and wants may align with God's plan and if this is the case, God will give it to us when He knows we need it or are ready for it. However, some of the things we think we need may not align to what God has planned for us. In the moments we realise this, we need to draw closer to God in prayer to gain understanding, desire what He knows we need and learn to be content in His provision and plan. The moment God's plan becomes sovereign in our lives, peace that surpasses all our understanding and contentment becomes ours. We become content because we know God and that He will:

- Provide for our needs
- Strengthen us
- Hear our prayers and,
- Give us peace

So, know God more, seek His will and plan. Realign and check the motives behind your wants through prayer and most importantly trust God that if that thing is truly for you, you will receive that thing at the perfect time because His plan and timing is sovereign (has supreme power and authority). We must surrender. And because He's loving, you'll start to enjoy your life more because you'll be living with freedom and no worry about what you do not have or what you may be missing out on. Hebrews 12:2 tells us to fix our eyes on Jesus because on the journey of life, there will be many distractions that may tempt us to compare our lives with others and become discontented. But we need to stay focused on Jesus and who He is: our provider and protector.

Whatever we need Him to be at that point in time. That's why He is the 'I Am that I Am', God is everything, so fix your eyes on Him.

Meditate:

What comes to your mind when thinking about your Decisions and Desires after today's study? Meditate and add anything that comes to your mind to the prayer list below.

Time to Pray:

- Thank you, Father, for your love and provision.
- I pray Lord, you will help me to be content in all things, not to compare or be influenced by the world's thinking, opinions, or desires.
- I pray for a mindset change, to have the mind of Christ and to overcome distractions by fixing my eyes on Jesus.
- I choose to surrender my plans, wants and needs to You, so You can be sovereign in my life.
- Father, I desire to know and seek You more.
- In Jesus' name, Amen.

"For to me to live is
Christ, and to die is gain."
Philippians 1:21

(Source: www.biblehub.com)

“You Can Do It!”

Day 26

Reading of the Day: Joshua 1.

"Be strong and of good courage" or "be courageous" is mentioned four times in this chapter. Three times, it's God's direct instruction to Joshua, and the fourth time, it's from the people of Israel, also to Joshua. Despite God already promising victory in verses 2-4, where He declares, "I've given you this land," Joshua still needed encouragement. This speaks to us in our life journeys too: even when we know God's promises or what we need to do, we often need a boost of courage and confidence to take the first step. It's a reminder that it's okay to not feel fully equipped—what matters is receiving encouragement from God and the support of those around us. Together, we are stronger than we realise.

Sidenote: isn't it interesting how God told Joshua three times and the people around him told him once. This encourages us that we need God more than anyone else. God's voice should be paramount, the priority, the loudest, the most important, the most frequent, the most sought after to encourage and direct us in all we do. Seeking God, remembering His word and promises is so important especially when we are stepping out doing something new or difficult. It becomes our foundation, our strength, our confidence. The more we hear and listen to Him, the better our journey is to fulfil His purpose.

Additionally, although the people around him who were Israelites said it once, what we can take from this is that we still need people around us to encourage us and urge us on. But how much better if it is people that will speak the word of God into our lives. They said the exact same thing God told Joshua. How amazing would it be for us to have people in our circle that are with us and love us, supporting our God given purposes and plans, who are also believers in God so allow themselves to be used by Him. This will only solidify the strength and will of God within us.

Back to the focus of today's devotional in being strong and courageous: what does this mean?

- Strong means powerful, not easily broken, or damaged, able to withstand force, pressure, or wear (Cambridge Dictionaries[4]).
- Courageous means not deterred by danger or pain, brave, overcomer and willing to act (Cambridge Dictionaries[5]).

Joshua needed this to be able to conquer and go into the promised land by war (verse 14-15), he needed to have strength to 'run and not be weary', being strong in mind, body and in spirit. He needed to be willing to take

4 https://dictionary.cambridge.org/dictionary/english/strong
5 https://dictionary.cambridge.org/dictionary/english/courageous

action and not be fearful when things were not making sense or didn't look like what God had promised. He had to be brave going into unknown territory and out of his comfort zone. God had to remind him, because God knew what was ahead of him and so laboured the encouragement for him to be strong and courageous.

Also, in chapter 1 God made so many promises so let's be reminded that it is important for us to hold on to any promises God has made with us including in His word. Keeping these promises in your memories and heart will enable you to live and be strong and courageous so you can fulfil your purpose. God's promises are Yes and Amen (2 Corinthians 1:20). Numbers 23:19 reminds us that God is not a man, that He should lie, or a son of man, that He should change His mind. Hold on to these promises to strengthen for what you have ahead of you today:

- Every place that the sole of your foot will tread upon I have given you, as I said to Moses.' (verse 3).
- No man shall be able to stand before you all the days of your life." (verse 5).
- As I was with Moses, so I will be with you." (verse 5).
- Have I not commanded you? Be strong and of good courage; do not be afraid, nor be dismayed, for the Lord your God is with you wherever you go." (verse 9).

Meditate

What comes to your mind when thinking about your Decisions and Desires after today's study? Meditate and add anything that comes to your mind to the prayer list below.

Time to Pray

- Thank You God for always being with me and for preparing me for what is ahead of me.
- I pray for Your voice to be sovereign in my life. May I seek You Father in everything I do, listening to Your voice above others through Your Word.
- To be surrounded by people that love God, are willing to be used by God.
- Lord, please continue to prepare me for what You have prepared for me.
- Help me Lord to be strong and courageous in You. Help me also to keep my eyes fixed on You so I won't backslide or be stagnant in fear of moving forward or enduring any discomfort.
- I pray for the power and willingness to seek You God and for a retentive memory from the Holy Spirit to hold on to Your promises from Your word as I live this life.

- Lord, please teach and show me how to have patient endurance.
- I ask for forgiveness for when I have had unbelief, listened, and followed bad advice or have sought the uncomplicated way out that is not God's plan.
- Help me to do and accept Your will so I can complete the tasks and purpose You have set out for me.
- Thank You God for Your love, patience, and goodness, and for never leaving me, forsaking me, or giving up on me.

I have personalised a prayer based on Joshua 1, added some words and omitted some verses:

The Lord will give me every place where I set my foot, as He promised Moses. No one will be able to stand against me all the days of my life. As the Lord was with Moses, so He will be with me. He will never leave me nor forsake me in all I do. I declare that I will be strong and very courageous, and I will be careful to obey all the law and word of God. I will not turn from it to the right or to the left, so that I may be successful wherever I go. In Jesus' name, Amen.

“For God so loved the world,
that he gave his only Son,
that whoever believes in
him should not perish but
have eternal life. For God
did not send his Son into
the world to condemn the
world, but in order that
the world might be saved
through him.”
John 3:16-17

(Source: www.biblehub.com)

Final Hopes and Thoughts

We've come to the end of this devotional, and my hope is that you've not only enjoyed spending time with God but that you've also learned, celebrated, or even felt challenged along the way. Each moment is an opportunity to bring glory to God, and I encourage you to continue diving into His Word. Let your decisions and desires reflect His will and keep loving God with all your heart and mind. May you be richly blessed in every area of your life, and may His peace guide you always. In Jesus' name, Amen.

Acknowledgments

First, I give all glory and thanks to God for the call He has placed on my life and for the gift of writing. I am deeply grateful for the courage and patience He has given me throughout this journey, and for never giving up on me, even when I doubted my own abilities.

To my family and friends—thank you for your unwavering encouragement and support. Your belief in me has been a constant source of strength. I am especially grateful to my Dad, who instilled in me a deep faith and a love for God's Word from a young age. I pray he can now see the fruits of his labour through this work.

A special thanks to Pastor Mike White for believing in this project and for supporting the creation of this book. Your guidance, faith, and encouragement have been instrumental in bringing this vision to life.

May God continue to bless each of you abundantly.

About the Author

Sarah is a devoted Christian who is based in London, UK. Known for her calm, coaching approach, she is passionate about helping others deepen their faith and truly know themselves and God. Decisions and Desires is her debut book, a collection of reflections and revelations drawn from her personal devotional time.

Her writing invites personal thought and hope, offering readers a fresh perspective on the Bible, personal development, and spiritual growth. When she's not writing, Sarah works in Human Resources, enjoys travelling, or spends time with friends and family. Follow her on social media @decisionsanddesires for updates and inspiration.

Printed in Dunstable, United Kingdom

63691851R00111